Losing It—Behaviors and Mindsets that Ruin Careers

Losing It—Behaviors and Mindsets that Ruin Careers

Lessons on Protecting Yourself from Avoidable Mistakes

Bill Lane

Vice President, Publisher: Tim Moore
Associate Publisher and Director of Marketing: Amy Neidlinger
Executive Editor: Jeanne Glasser Levine
Editorial Assistant: Tamara Hummel
Development Editor: Russ Hall
Operations Specialist: Jodi Kemper
Assistant Marketing Manager: Megan Graue
Cover Designer: Alan Clements
Managing Editor: Kristy Hart
Project Editor: Betsy Harris
Copy Editor: Krista Hansing Editorial Services, Inc.
Proofreader: Leslie Joseph
Senior Indexer: Cheryl Lenser
Compositor: Nonie Ratcliff
Manufacturing Buyer: Dan Uhrig

© 2012 by Bill Lane
Published by Pearson Education, Inc.
Publishing as FT Press
Upper Saddle River, New Jersey 07458

FT Press offers excellent discounts on this book when ordered in quantity for bulk purchases or special sales. For more information, please contact U.S. Corporate and Government Sales, 1-800-382-3419, corpsales@pearsontechgroup.com. For sales outside the U.S., please contact International Sales at international@pearsoned.com.

Company and product names mentioned herein are the trademarks or registered trademarks of their respective owners.

Printed in the United States of America

First Printing May 2012

ISBN-10: 0-13-304024-0
ISBN-13: 978-0-13-304024-1

Pearson Education LTD.
Pearson Education Australia PTY, Limited.
Pearson Education Singapore, Pte. Ltd.
Pearson Education Asia, Ltd.
Pearson Education Canada, Ltd.
Pearson Educación de Mexico, S.A. de C.V.
Pearson Education—Japan
Pearson Education Malaysia, Pte. Ltd.

Library of Congress Cataloging-in-Publication Data

Lane, Bill, 1944-
  Losing it : behaviors and mindsets that ruin careers : lessons on protecting yourself from avoidable mistakes / Bill Lane. -- 1st ed.
    p. cm.
  ISBN 978-0-13-304024-1 (hardcover : alk. paper)
  1. Leadership. 2. Management--Psychological aspects. 3. Business ethics. I. Title.
  HD57.7.L364 2012
  658.4'092--dc23

                        2012008147

For Beth. Forever. And for our crown jewels:
Bill, Regan, and Tom.

Contents

Acknowledgments

I would like to express my deep appreciation to the many important people—some unnamed—who spent their valuable time with me, not just out of friendship, but in the hope that some of their insights and experiences might help someone, someday, avoid "losing it" in the life game of leadership that they have chosen to play.

About the Author

Bill Lane is a native of Brooklyn, New York, and has degrees from Niagara University and Northern Arizona University. He served as a Green Beret officer in Vietnam in 1968–69 and later worked as a congressional liaison officer and speechwriter at the Pentagon for seven years. He was appointed Manager of Executive Communications at General Electric and spent nearly 20 years as Jack Welch's speechwriter; he retired in 2002.

Bill's first book, *Jacked Up: How Jack Welch Talked GE into Becoming the World's Greatest Company,* was named one of the "Best Business Books of the Year" by *Strategy+Business.*

He writes and lives in Easton, Connecticut.

Introduction

"Only a fool learns from his own mistakes. A wise man learns from the mistakes of others."
—Bismarck

If this book ever sees the light of other eyes than mine, I can guarantee that someone will ask, "What made you write it?" As the nightmarish beast-villain in *No Country for Old Men* verbally smirked, "They all say that...."

I wrote it not only to satisfy a not-totally-justified, and never satisfied, ego, but to see if I could help people with observations gleaned from more than 30 years in government and industry on what accelerates personal success and what kills it.

I began this book with what I thought was a catchy and appropriate working title, *Trainwrecks and Turnarounds,* and set forth with a vision of doing good by painting accurate, semitragic sketches of good, successful, "fast-track" people whose careers imploded or were bombed into oblivion by character or personality flaws that they failed to correct. To balance these dismal accounts, I intended to showcase some inspirational stories of those who got off the canvas and soared to new heights of success and glory by recognizing their flaws and weaknesses, correcting them, and moving on.

I thought that made for a neat and helpful premise for my work—but it didn't hold up very long in the cruel light of introspection and after conversations with more than a few brilliant and successful people. Oh, the train wreck analogy was fertile ground for mining; the carcasses and debris of losers who did not *have* to be losers are all over the place. People who used to fly into Harry Truman Airport in the Virgin Islands, as I did every now and then as both a pilot and a passenger seated in the back, used to advise their friends not to look out the window until after landing and taxi-out. The approach was tricky, and both sides of the runway had burned-out wrecks and scattered debris marring the landscaping. Whether this tragic junk was left there because of bureaucratic inertia or as a warning was never clear, but the cockpit was usually quiet until the plane stopped safely.

The wreckage was a graphic and effective warning. That is what I hope this book to be, too: both graphic and effective.

The seed for this book was planted in my mind eight years ago. I had been fired—I'm sorry, I had *retired*—from General Electric, and at the tender age of 57, I set out to make my way in the world. I intended to enable my three high-school kids and young first wife to some day financially step over my decaying, martini-saturated carcass—fresh from yet another pathetic performance on the golf course—and move on.

So I set out to become a "freelance" speechwriter, a gig that pays well when you get work. Something I've been successful at, having had my craft forged and tested in the flames of 20 years working with Jack Welch of General Electric, probably the greatest and most demanding CEO in business history.

One of my early clients was a guy named Jack Shaw, an engineer who was quite older than I was; he's now the retired president and CEO of Hughes Electronics in southern California. Shaw's speech was for a graduation at the University of Maryland, and he agreed to a quiet, country-boy, engineer-type speech.

In my view, the only good graduation speeches are the ones that sent the pimply-faced sex maniacs off into the world with at least *one thought* they would remember 20 years later—or at least 20 *minutes* later. Most graduation speeches do neither.

I don't remember the message of my college graduation speaker, or even who he or she was. I'm not even sure I was present. I don't know, maybe I was.

To be fair to this mysterious speaker, I was probably hung over (if I was there). I think my parents were there. What I'm telling you is, of course, total hyperbole. Of course my parents were there—and so was I. However, I truly have no idea who gave the speech. But if something was said that amounted to any insight or interesting perspective, I probably would have remembered it.

One speech I will never forget—although I was not there to hear it, of course—was General MacArthur's speech to the cadets at West Point. It combined beautiful, lyrical English with solid advice on cultivating in oneself a leadership code that would advantage anyone, in any lifetime endeavor:

> They teach you to be proud and unbending in honest failure, but humble and gentle in success; not to substitute words for action; not to seek the path of comfort, but to face the stress and spur of difficulty and challenge; to learn to stand up in the storm, but to have compassion on those who fail; to master yourself before you seek to master others; ...to reach into the future yet never neglect the past; to be serious, but never take yourself seriously...."[1]

Shaw showed that he had "mastered" himself early in our conversation during my L.A. visit to frame his speech, and he startled me with a modest, ineffably wise, and instructive observation.

Shaw had begun a career at Hughes after an "undistinguished" (his description) four years at Purdue. He told me that, after a few years, he realized "a lot of people...were simply better engineers than [he] was."

He continued, "But what I did well—where I shone, as it turned out—was in my willingness to appraise my weaknesses and strengths and act on that data. Had I tried to mimic the success paths of other engineers and scientists, without possessing their gifts, I might have faded into mediocrity and oblivion, if I didn't get into another line of work.

"What I discovered about myself was that I had a great work ethic. I could lead. I could organize. I could manage. I could get things done. I found that quite a few of the technical people I worked with were not good at doing those kinds of things.

"So I focused on becoming a manager, a leader of scientists and engineers, and one of the first things I found out—very pleasantly—was that those who can get things done tend to get paid more than those who can't, or don't choose to."

This, in my view, is a stunning piece of self-evaluation and mature decisiveness on the part of a young man—rare, in my experience (and something I'd never really experienced in my own life) and almost unheard of in older, established people.

The ability to look at oneself in a cold, unflattering, florescent-lit mirror; evaluate what you see; and act on that evaluation is a faculty that can and must be cultivated if your train is to stay on its track—and accelerate.

This is not a conventional self-help tome. I have no human resources experience and certainly no psychology training in my background. My intention is to outline some behaviors I have witnessed in otherwise brilliant and successful people that have brought them down and ruined them. I also outline the few cases of people who have turned their lives around after crashing and burning.

If crusty old Jack Shaw of Hughes gave me at least an inkling that a book such as this might have some merit or utility, Tom Coughlin, head coach of the New York Giants, provided me with a shining example of a turnaround, a self-redemption that pushed me over the edge of rumination and into a flurry of pen-and-yellow-pad activity.

Two years ago, Coughlin, in his very early 60s, was presiding over a looming disaster: His team, loaded with talent, limped into the playoffs each year and lost in the first round. Coughlin was clearly on the way out. The players hated his ranting and screaming. He embarrassed his family, all watching at home, with his arm-waving and red-faced shouting on the sidelines as he badgered and humiliated players who were already embarrassed by failure. He seemed a doomed dinosaur, taking an unhappy team down with him into the tar pit of yet another failed season.

But before training camp for the 2007–08 season, he looked at himself in the baleful light of the mirror—and through the sullen eyes of his players—and decided that something had to change. *He* was that something. Michael Strahan, a defensive back and a great player (old by NFL standards) had said before the season opened, "I can't play with this man. He's crazy!"[2]

On February 3, 2008, the Super Bowl champion Giants dumped a large bucket of Gatorade over the head of a coach they would have been more inclined to *hit* over the head only a few months earlier.

Asked in the afterglow of the miraculous Super Bowl victory of February 2008, "Has the coach really changed?" Strahan said, "Yeah, he's smiling. He's using the word fun and enjoyment...and it blows my mind." Strahan went on to say, "He still has his rules.... We respect those rules. But as a person, his demeanor in the locker room is a lot more at ease. At practice, he still demands the best of you. After practice, if it's not the greatest practice, he doesn't jump down your throat. He'll say, 'That's not the caliber of practice we need to be champions. We need to come out with more energy and have more fun. That blows my mind, but it has worked. I think he has definitely changed and it's real and it's for the better."[3]

Coughlin had changed, deliberately, purposefully, and, yes, superficially in some respects. He even went bowling with the team he used to scream at. He kept his rules, principles, tenets, and discipline, but he rid himself of the behaviors that would have brought down the inexorable personal and collective mantle of "loser" over the heads and shoulders of the Giants and their coach.

He turned it around and triumphed. And then, amazingly, he did it again in February 2012 by winning his second Super Bowl. And all the people who were predicting the ash heap for the end of his career—me included—began to speculate about the possibility of Coughlin being inducted into the Hall of Fame.

The point: Set your mind to changing, if you think you need to. This book will help you decide *whether you do need to change*.

Consider a warning: A woman I admire and respect opined of my last book, *Jacked Up,* that although she liked it, it was "all over the place." This one is probably worse, ranging from Cicero, to the pre–Civil War era, to the *Titanic,* to Dwight D. Eisenhower, to Ronald Reagan, to Jack Welch, and to a cast of hundreds—or at least dozens. It investigates why some people succeeded, why some people lost it, and how some people did both.

But first, here's an important question and, I hope, a serious answer. The important question came from Mark Vachon, now vice president and head of the massive "Ecomagination" effort at GE. Vachon said to me as I began to pick his fertile brain, "Bill, before we get started, what exactly do you mean by 'losing'?"

In my view, there are two kinds of potential losers: big-player losers and mid- to lower-level losers.

Big-player losers, made up of senior management, including CEO's, seldom *really* lose, except in the ego department (and I don't minimize the trauma and distress that entails). But if they mess up, they usually "bounce" to another big job, either within the company (which is unusual) or to another major gig. Often they become the CEO of another company, generally with an increase in pay. Bob Nardelli went from a highly successful run at GE to Home Depot and scored an enormous, stupendous pay package. He screwed up and was canned by the board. Was he then consigned to the ash heap and the unemployment line? Not exactly. He moved on to sit in Lee Iacocca's old chair as the CEO of Chrysler!

Similarly, Carly Fiorina messed up at Hewlett-Packard and was canned. Did she retreat into obscurity? Not exactly. She made a very serious run for the United States Senate. She wasn't successful on election day, but I guarantee you she will be heard from again.

That's how big-player losers blow it. They are cats that inevitably land on their feet, sometimes with bruised egos, but they're not dining in dumpsters.

Then we have the mid- to lower-level professionals who fail. They don't do so well.

They get fired—or retired, like me. The younger ones, typically in their 30s or 40s, are often seriously unemployed and roam the depressing "networking" sessions hoping to meet people they can email later, telling them how much they "enjoyed meeting" them (even if they felt the exact opposite) and asking to be "kept in mind" for any future opportunities.

If they do find something, it's often at an insultingly lower pay level than their former gig paid.

I tend to fit partly into that category: mid-executive level, fortunately at an age to get me on a "bridge" to retirement, with a gentle push from "Generous Electric"—and sufficient resources from the fortuitous concatenation of munificent stock option grants and the 15-year market rush of the mid-1980s and the roaring '90s.

GE owed me nothing.

I called my wife, began to clear out my desk, and walked out the door whistling.

Most people don't.

You may not, either.

Endnotes

1. http://www.nationalcenter.org/MacArthurFarewell.html.

2. Michael Eisen, "The New Look Coach Couglin," http://origin-www.giants.com/news/headlines/story.asp?story_id=26899.

3. Michael Eisen, "The New Look Coach Couglin," http://origin-www.giants.com/news/headlines/story.asp?story_id=26899.

1

Losing It

Mailin' It In, Starring the Coasters, with a Guest Appearance by One-Trick Pony

I may as well get my story out on the table before I start pontificating about others. Irving Berlin once said, "The toughest thing about being a success is that you've got to keep on being a success."

In the late 1990s, on a beautiful Connecticut summer afternoon, my cell phone went off in the Grill Room of Brooklawn, the idyllic old country club I frequented. I was finishing a two- or three-beer lunch before teeing it up with "the boys," 50ish dudes like myself. It was my secretary "Mr. Welch called. Would you call him?" "Sure." I knew this was not going to be a high-tension deal, as many Welch calls were. I had been Jack Welch's speechwriter and communications manager for about 18 years at the time. I had just finished—or helped Jack finish—a magnificent presentation. I knew I wasn't on the dreaded Welch shit list, as I had been when caught sneaking out during work hours twice in one week. (That had produced a spectacular explosion of vitriol and profanity that I chronicled in horrific detail in my last book. But being the "kid" I imagined I still was, I figured Welch had "sneaked out" enough in his nearly 40-year career to carry a low-single-digit handicap. So he sort of understood.)

On one occasion, Welch had me paged while I was firing my .357 at an indoor range ten minutes from GE, in Monroe, Connecticut. Since I was "on the clock" at the range, I was paying for the time I should have been blasting on the range with two or three other knuckleheads, and my time was instead being occupied by the chairman of GE with some annoying concern. I was "riding high" at the time (that is, doing well), an evaluation that I could read in Welch's face and voice more reliably than in anyone else's "evaluation." I mock-angrily asked Welch if he had nothing better to do than spy on his minions leaving the beautiful GE corporate campus and then harass them individually.

Welch thought this was moderately amusing. He was in a great mood, as he often was, and he was in another friendly and jovial mood when he called me in the Grill Room of Brooklawn that day. "Bill, it went great. Best pitch on the program. Warren [Buffet] wants a copy. Loved it. Great job. Just wanted to tell you." Wonderful. I purred.

And then the liquid nitrogen of career doom ran down my spine as the CEO of the world's greatest—and, at the time, most valuable—company laughed as he prepared to hang up and said, "You can go back to sleep now."

I was stunned. I knew exactly what he had said but cut off one of his "Ha-ha's" with "What did you just say?"

"Just kiddin'. Great job. See ya ...."

Not kidding. His words were benign and affectionate, but if ever a cockpit voice had uttered an eerie, urgent warning, this was it. "Career ascent over. Flaps down. Prepare for terrain impact." This was it.

As I said earlier, I was in my 50s and, like several of my colleagues, was rudimentarily competent in e-mail and web surfing but ignorant of the explosive world-changing significance of the Internet. Worse, I was contemptuous of many of the Internet's devotees and zealots. We mocked the barely-30-somethings who spoke in what we thought was affected jargon, and we aped the silly, neobohemian knock-off e-culture. In a way, we took satisfaction from the dot-com meltdown at the turn of the century, crowing that we (I, mostly) had called it bullshit all along.

But the dot-com apers had it right—at least, ballpark right—and they were the future, especially in their not-particularly-high-paid games. I was running out the string of my (high-paid) game and was flaps down, not by choice, with black clouds looming on the horizon. It all dated from the "go back to sleep" comment from Welch that lit up, with terrifying vividness, the end of my career.

Oh, I made a stab at trying to get current, much like in an old *Honeymooners* segment, the one where Ralph Kramden puts on a pathetically stretched and antique high-school letter-sweater and takes his wife, Alice, to the roller-skating rink, only to fall on his ass, all in an attempt to regain his lost youth and get "with it" again. GE had given me an IBM Workbook, a $4,000 item at the time, and I'd brought it home to show the kids and play golf games. I gave it back to the company when I got bored and felt guilty.

Dinosaur Diary

Don't get me wrong. What I did for a living was relatively important, helping Welch with his communications—speeches, CEO annual report letters, presentations, and the like. I ran the major company meetings, taught communications at GE's world-famous management school, and made a very decent amount of money (mostly from stock options).

Sounds like I had a fair and productive amount of stuff on the plate of a midlevel guy who was not a superstar. I did everything asked of me—and did it well. But as the 1990s waned, Welch was beginning the preliminary victory laps of his fabulous tenure, with retirement announced and pending. He needed me less than he had in earlier days. I now reported to a new vice president, a young woman Welch had brought in from NBC, and she had a suspected mandate from him to clean house in corporate communications.

At a sit-down, I was told that I needed to "do more" to merit the significant compensation I was taking home (once again, based on stock options). "What do you *want* me to do?" I asked. I got vague answers in return. If conversations along these lines occur when you are in your 50s, 40s, 30s, or 20s, you could be in extreme trouble career wise and need to take radical action immediately. I should have confronted Welch with my perceived unfairness of what was being done and demand to know what "more" I could do. He liked that kind of thing and dreaded, as he often said, being "unfair." He probably would have responded to the challenge, and I might have gotten things back on track. Maybe.

It's generally too late at that point.

As I said, and I think I'm being objective, I did everything I was told to do—and did it well. But it *wasn't enough,* and I crashed and burned at 57. I walked away from my beloved GE with a few pangs, but mostly laughing. Had I been much younger, it would have been a possibly avoidable calamity for me and my family.

In "Year T minus 2" (*T* meaning "termination"), my V.P. boss walked into my office with my bonus envelope. At GE, it's called "incentive compensation" and is awarded to everyone eligible on the closest thing to a secular feast day in the company. Her face told a story. I took the sealed check document from her and held it by the corner, as one would an envelope containing a stool specimen. "Is this flat?" I asked. ("Flat" means no increase from last year, a bad biopsy report on a career in a company where increases were as predictable as peristalsis, which led Welch to sneeringly describing the bonus system as "another dental plan.")

"Yes," she said. "You need to do more."

"What more do you want me to do?" I ticked off some of the things I had added to my plate in recent months, which were dismissed as being "not that important."

You can—or should—see the futility and inevitable consequences of these pathetic conversations. The train was beginning to wobble toward derailment. The clock was now ticking, and despite a few rallies of several months' duration, usually associated with triumphs in helping Welch communicate (which he actually did masterfully and naturally), the two-year slide to "T minus zero" was now inexorable. (When I was at the Pentagon during a previous seven-year career, the standard derisive description of an aging, less-than-productive officer, usually a lieutenant colonel, was that he had "retired in place.")

Welch was retiring, and his successor, Jeff Immelt, said he didn't want a speechwriter. That left me a beached, overcompensated minnow—or maybe large-mouthed bass.

Classifying myself as a "loser" for the purpose of mere neatness and self-effacement in this book would not be totally fair, either to me or to you. I walked out with a great package, a pretty fair pile in the bank, and few regrets. But after a few months of bad golf, early martinis, and trips to GE wearing a "Retiree" badge (which for me produced vague visions of the Living Dead of Romero's famous black-and-white-nightmare), stumbling along from the fitness center, to the employee store for GE light bulbs, to the medical center for free flu shots, and then up to my old office corridor to see old friends who had other things to do than commune with the undead, I began to ruminate on what I had done right and *wrong* in my latter years at GE.

I *had* coasted. I'd done everything perfectly and had kept the boss, Welch, happy. But I needed to have done "more." The best advice I can give anyone in management in business, organizations, politics, the military, or life in general is to fight and strive endlessly to expand your responsibilities and *never* stop, *never* coast, *never* get comfortable, no matter how many people tell you how great you are and how well you are doing.

Warships in wartime (and wartime is all the time in business) vary in speeds and headings toward their destination. A steady cruise, even at high speed, invites the attentions of periscopes (see the U.S.S. *Indianapolis*). Cultivate indispensability. Keep changing. Keep impressing yourself and others. "Show off" with actions, never words.

When dealing with very senior people, particularly CEOs, all of us have wondered at some time, "How did this guy get this job? He (or she) seems pretty run-of-the-mill to me."

My first impression of the aforementioned Jack Shaw of Hughes was that he should have had a long weed sticking out of his mouth. He had a vaguely cornpone yet pleasant manner with a self-effacing Southern-boy affect (or what I thought was an affect) that was hard to get used to after a 20-year dose of the frenetic, hyperactive, and hyperintelligent Jack Welch. I thought, "Okay, he's a nice guy. I'll work with him, do his speech, and pick up my check. But I'm not sure how much of substance he'll have to say."

In retrospect, he said a lot, some of which I pass on to you in the way of advice. *His* advice had come too late for me: "[M]ore important than any of the rest, you need to ask yourself *every day of your career*, 'Am I up to speed? Am I pushing the envelope, or am I stagnating and falling behind?'"

Shaw advocated being "absolutely paranoid" (how's that for advice?) about the currency of your technical knowledge, as well as the currency of your grasp of what you're working at every day. I would add the observation that you should be fearful if you see the team getting together on the project without you or saying, "We can handle this, Mary—you don't need to waste your afternoon. It's a lot of IT stuff." What you may be hearing is another version of, "You can go back to sleep."

Don't let it come to that.

Shaw spoke of mid-50s people (or older) coming to work every day and pushing into unknown, virgin territory. These people, visceral and instinctive winners, cultivated an obsession with staying at the front edge of "what's going on."

Shaw told me, with affection and admiration for some engineers in their 50s and 60s, that "they cultivated a mind-set of staying 'with it' to the point that they actually ask to leave a project in its final successful stages, a satisfying time most people enjoy, and let others 'mop up' and get much of the applause, because a new train is leaving for the unknown and they want to be on it" (instead of *under* it, I guess). The right people, and everyone else who counts, will know and value your focus on the future.

I sort of wrapped up Shaw's speech with a thought Welch expressed incessantly over the years: "Never come out for a second or third bow when the world is waiting for the next act." Otherwise, you're a candidate for the lethal "one trick pony" sobriquet. George Jamison of Spencer Stuart described the plight of a senior executive (one of his search firm's clients) who had justifiably made an industry-wide name for himself for a fresh and clever marketing philosophy. When his company was acquired, he was squeezed out, only to be snapped up by another company, which, in turn, was dissolved. He then found himself hunting for a third time. His part in interviews with other companies that were initially interested was to expand on the marketing philosophy for which he was moderately known and respected. The verdict? "One-trick pony. Living off the same achievement for 20 years. No new thoughts."

No new job.

The one-trick syndrome is an eventual career killer—usually, but not always. All of us are familiar with the Tom Peters, Search-For-Excellence types who come up with a striking theory of management or a quirky, brilliant, captivating look at human behavior;

shoot to fame and success; and then beat the same old tired nag (or some permutation of it) to death. They drive their audiences and readers to eye-rolling or eye-closing. I'm picking on Peters because, although he favorably reviewed my last book, he found my descriptions of GE culture "toxic" and claimed he "threw the book down" several times. But other examples come to mind as well.

Coldplay, a talented and popular group who did a haunting, evocative, and sad song called "When I Ruled the World—Viva La Vida," now churns out songs that, although not bad, all sound to me like permutations of the original. In contrast, the Beatles, Billy Joel, Elton John, and Talking Heads, are all delightfully all over the place—unpredictable, new, and fresh.

In my own case, when I began to shop around the idea of this book, I was asked pointedly whether this was "another Welch book." My agent and old friend Leah Spiro told me that my "base" had eroded; Welch had been out of GE for years and, although still visible on TV, no longer had the cache of his GE years or evoked interest. I needed to move on.

My observation is that you should move like a pinball around the arena of ideas, without changing the underlying beliefs that guide you (unless you come to see them as erroneous or in need of modification). Tom Coughlin of my Giants didn't. He just started smiling and kidding, kicked ass in private, and took the team bowling.

To put it in GE terms, Jeff Immelt was quoted in the book *Jeff Immelt and the New GE Way* as saying, "I think longevity [read: survival] is a function of two things. It's a function of performance and your own ability to reinvent yourself."[1]

Welch was late to the information age. In the 1980s, I vividly remember Welch announcing to his officers that the expense of computers was getting "out of hand" and that, henceforth, only a company officer could authorize the purchase of a personal computer for use by anyone.

Once we characterized the information technology function as something that was "formerly the abode of failed finance managers." Actually, it was. But even then, I, a computer moron, had a glimpse of a dinosaur poking his head out of the primordial pit and making a loud, primitive noise.

Welch quickly refreshed his opinion—as he had an uncanny ability to do—and became a rabid, foaming fanatic of anything "e." Three or four years later, while he was having makeup applied for a video with CFO Dennis Dammerman, he was tormenting me on being "computer illiterate." I denied it because I had improved my skills considerably—well, maybe not that much. "Yeah, but can you do spreadsheets?" he asked, towel around his shoulders as makeup plaster was being applied. "No," I said, "I don't *need* to do spreadsheets."

"*I* can do spreadsheets," he claimed, like a little kid.

I asked Dennis Dammerman, also with towel around his neck as makeup was being applied, "How much are we paying this guy to do spreadsheets?"

On Welch's part, all this was cheerleading for something for which he had no real affinity yet knew would be a big part of the future of his company. Most of what he was saying was posturing, in a good sense, but he was smart enough to know how much he needed to be on top of a wave that will gather strength for the rest of our lives.

Warren Buffett, a great friend and fan of Welch, sent me a gracious email (which I show people like a child) about my last book and, specifically, a passage about him and Welch. It was clear that he had dictated the email to his assistant, who had sent it to me. Buffett is clearly not an IT acolyte. But I have a feeling that, at this point, he is beyond vulnerability to disaster—he's "playing the back nine" as I am, but with the extraordinary mind, personality, and wealth I will never acquire.

When I joined GE in my 30s, at the same time that Welch became CEO, I met and worked with three kinds of people.

The first group was typically mid-50s and had grown up under two or three nationally celebrated and revered CEOs. They loathed, feared, and privately ridiculed Welch: his ideas, his brashness, his reputed "wildness" with the plastics business, even his stuttering, which was fairly severe at that time. (He outgrew nearly all of this over the years, except for some of the wildness.) Their gloomy and dire predictions of the company's bleak future under this maniac amused me at first, but I soon realized that they were casting themselves in the role of the worn furniture in a house being prepared for a major remodeling; their destination of "the curb" became increasingly obvious.

Those who were within reasonable range of retirement were allowed to go about their appointed rounds, as long as they didn't engage in the public carping, grumbling, and denigration of Welch and where he wanted to take this already successful company. They were eventually "packaged up," as I was decades later, or allowed to stumble over the finish line of 60—depressed, unhappy, bitter, and miserable, but secure.

Keith Sherin, a current vice chairman and CFO of GE, told me as we worked on a speech to the graduating MBAs of Notre Dame (his alma mater) that he had never seen a successful executive, at any level, with a "consistent gloom-and-doom attitude."

He compared Welch's attitudinal worldview with Jeffrey Immelt's. Welch's was characterized by some mercurial swings—a dip into a black funk at some occurrence or report or at the loss of a key player. (He claimed in his book that he ran into the bathroom and puked when apprised of Joe Jett's perfidy at GE's ill-starred and now-defunct brokerage firm Kidder Peabody). His other side was wild ebullience and soaring optimism. I remember him years ago getting in my face when GE had posted its first $5 billion earnings year: "What do you think of that, huh?" Laughing, levitating.

Immelt, whom I have known for many years but only casually, is consistently optimistic and remains so even in the face of the sagging stock price and semi-depression-plagued financial business exposure. Never a discouraging word. That's almost always a plus, except for one negative facet of the mindset I mention in the next chapter.

Sherin advised the MBAs to "cultivate a mindset of optimism, one that lights up the conference room when you walk in." Fake it, if you have to, but be wildly, enthusiastically supportive of the direction of the business or organization. Register reasoned, fact-buttressed reservations about some of its aspects, but never doubt the central premise or direction outlined by the leadership. If you think it's total bullshit, leave. If you can't afford to leave, "get your mind right," as Paul Newman was advised in *Cool Hand Luke*. After all, the leader may be right. Sometimes leaders actually are.

Above all, never become typecast as what I heard Larry Bossidy of GE and Honeywell call one of "the whispering cynics by the water cooler."

Change. "Sign on" to the program, even if you have reservations. Be a fanatic. Reinvent yourself. There's nothing evil about faking enthusiasm when the top dog vouchsafes a new initiative or idea. Grab it, run with it, tout it. Maybe he or she is right. If it turns into a mess, you have done above-and-beyond service to a lost cause.

Gary Reiner, a very young recruit from a GE fountain of youth, the Boston Consulting Group, came into our company as the vice president of business development in the late 1980s and could have forged a terrific career in that niche for a decade or even two. Instead, he kept reinventing himself, staying beyond current, leading Welch rather than padding along behind him. He had the intellect to do it, but more important, he had the instinct.

And that instinct, maybe counterintuitively, can be duplicated.

When Welch accepted without question his friend Larry Bossidy's (then CEO of Honeywell, after a huge career at GE) advice that Six Sigma methodology and culture worked, he signed on with typical fanaticism. And Reiner grabbed the franchise and ran with it, computer skills and high intelligence being no hindrance. After Welch was baptized belatedly into e-religion in the latter 1990s, Reiner was already deeply and comfortably conversant with the Internet and was already rolling with it. Bingo: senior vice president and chief information officer.

Reiner, the reinventor, was never on cruise control and never (at least in public) a cynic. His foot was always on the accelerator.

Stay on the edge, even if, to you, it seems forced and even phony. Sign on to do stuff you really don't understand, if it makes at least a modicum of sense to you. Act like a benevolent nut and fanatic. Stay on the edge. Some of us had reservations about Six Sigma and, frankly, didn't understand half the stuff we were immersed in, like the lengthy, compulsory training sessions, but we kept our mouths shut. It turned out that Bossidy, Welch, and Reiner were right. Six Sigma turned out to be a discipline and way of thinking suited for the entire company.

Once again, grumbling at the morning meeting and griping in the dark about "new stuff" are the activities of a doomed dinosaur, regardless of age. Confess your ignorance and show a strong desire to learn. Ask a subordinate or friend to spend some time with you and help you learn. They will generally be thrilled that you think that much of them. Most good people have a good teacher within them, eager to come out.

Grab it. Learn it. Run with it!

The ultimate sustainable advantage in your career is the ability to learn.

Endnote

1. David Magee, *Jeff Immelt and the New GE Way: Innovation, Transformation, and Winning in the 21st Century* (New York: McGraw-Hill, 2009), 47.

2

The Integrity Trap and Opportunity

Cheats and Freaks and Sneaks and Sleazes—and Good Guys Who Tiptoe into the Gray Zone

Deliberate and calculated dishonesty, stealing, and sleaziness are behaviors we can all piously condemn as we rend our garments Pharisee style. It makes us feel good or at least superior to evil cheaters. But are these people born rotten? Is anyone? Maybe. But Hitler, in *Mein Kampf*, recounts feeding starving mice crumbs of bread from his own meager food in his youth—mostly out of amusement, but at least partly out of pity and empathy. How did he get from there to...wherever?

The cesspool that was Enron has been overchronicled, but are we to believe that these Wharton, Harvard, and Columbia 25-year-old super-achiever energy traders were born evil? Sucked lying and economic rapine from their mothers' breasts? Were taught by evil, swashbuckling college professors to do things like screw large areas of the country with manipulated power outages and brownouts?

Maybe a couple of natural-born low-lifes fall into the mix, but I doubt the whole crowd was infected with the sleaze-gene described by Bethany McLean and Peter Elkind in *The Smartest Guys in the Room*. Best guess: They were mostly decent men and women who became marinated in the stew of a culture of smash-and-grab greed and amorality that they stepped into the day they walked in the door at Enron—and Enron skimmed a fair amount of the cream of the biz schools. GE got a lot of the rest, and the management of our company would never have considered any-thing like what went on in the Enron sewer. I don't say that piously or self-righteously. Such employees would have been fired and committed to an institution had they even suggested cheating or doing something sleazy, because we were told we might destroy a unique American institution if we ever did—and we believed that because it was true.

When did the "kids'" awareness of sleaze begin? When did they sign on? Probably not on Day 1. Or possibly on Day 1, if they had imbibed that "Masters of the Universe" crap that spread from Wall Street like bubonic plague over a fair bit of American business. And the thoroughly rotten leadership of the company encouraged their derring-do and corrosive cynicism.

Develop a Good Sense of Tumor

I have sometimes—often, actually, and morbidly—wondered how a malignant tumor is born. At what hour of the day—when riding a motorcycle, sleeping, having lunch, making love—does a *single cell* go bad, go nuts, do something invisible to only a micro-scope that is so destructive that it has the capacity to kill the entire body?

Wouldn't it be useful if you had a flag come up on your mental dashboard that beeped and said, "At 2:47 a.m. on February 9, five hours ago, a melanoma cell split and went off the reservation and is now loose in your system. We are attempting to locate it, but please see your physician immediately. Thank you."

I have no doubt that, within decades, the human body will be "wired," with minimal discomfort, with sensors that can be monitored through the skin and displayed, say, while you brush your teeth, to warn you of any anomalies you need to keep an eye on or have checked.

However, as far as business success, careers, and life in general go, one bright red flag *is*, or should be, plainly visible on the dashboard of your soul.

I spent some time with an old friend, Dave Calhoun, formerly the vice chairman of GE and now the "78 Million Dollar Man"[1]—that is, the CEO of Nielsen. We kicked around this and other issues as we prepared for his graduation address to 25,000 of his fellow alumnae and their families at Virginia Tech commencement a year or two before the insane violence that befell that great old school.

Calhoun told me, "There may come a day in your career when you are asked to approve, or go along with, or wink at, or ignore something that, if you do go along with it, will have a positive impact on some measure or metric that you are judged on.

"You may know that day, that you and your colleagues are *near the edge*. The lawyers or 'compliance people' may say 'It's okay,' or 'It shouldn't be a problem,' or 'That's the way they do it in the insurance industry'—or do business in China, or Hungary, or wherever." (Or you may hear the ugliest three words in any decision discussion: "Everybody does it.")

"But you must understand that when you are conscious that you are near the edge, that line in the sand, that line in your soul, is moving *closer* to you, not farther away, and you must have the faith in your own character and reputation and the courage to say, 'Hell, no! We're not doing this. And if you do it, you're doing it without me. And I'm picking up the phone.' Then you can go home and look your family in the eye and sleep like a baby. And there's nothing more important in any career you choose than the ability to do that...."

This reminds me of a well known scene from literature, "The boys turned in," as Mark Twain wrote in *The Adventures of Tom Sawyer*, "and slept the sleep of the conscience-free and the weary."

According to the book *The Smartest Guys in the Room*, Enron, on the other hand, began "turning to aggressive accounting tactics, tactics that planted those dangerous seeds. The things Enron did in those early years were not illegal, but they did help mask certain unpleasant financial realities, and they pushed the company into accounting's gray zone."

This chapter is not a sermon on the obvious by a pure spirit. But there's more than the obvious facets to the integrity issue. In my view, and the view of the serious business leaders I have spoken with, you must hold a moral, ethical compass as you move through your business or career life. As Dave Calhoun offered (and I wrote), you must cultivate an explosion of "dashboard lights" (not *a la* Meatloaf) when something you are contemplating or being ordered to do has an odor that troubles you or makes you uncomfortable—even *slightly* uncomfortable.

People who lie, cheat, or steal, or tolerate those who do, generally come to ruin in the business world, in the military, in institutions, in marriages, and in other familial relationships. George Jamison, my headhunter friend, says it definitively, but I can't prove that, knowing intuitively that some rats out there have gotten over the finish line with "intact" marriages and wealthy retirements.

Statistically, some people *must* get away with it.

I suppose I did, to a minor and venial degree in the Army in Vietnam. As an executive officer on a green beret "A team," I had, among my duties, the responsibility for signing for a duffel bag of Vietnamese *piastres* once a month and paying the Vietnamese and tribal mercenaries we accompanied on operations and advised. I "supervised" the payments at a table in the camp as the "strikers," a band of brave Vietnamese men, came up to collect their pittance. I knew that bribes, kickbacks, and other under-the-table-stuff was going on, but I understood little Vietnamese and didn't really care. The Vietnamese culture was corrupt to the core, as far as I could tell.

But "when in Rome".... I had my own game working. When one or five or ten of the strikers were killed, I was to authorize the payment of a "death gratuity" (sounds like a tip) to their families, typically a princely sum of $100 or so. Sometimes I bent some of my primitive accounting rules and gave several times that to some real heroes. One was a horribly smallpox-scarred sergeant named Yao who probably saw more combat than some American Medal of Honor winners who had wound up getting shot and paralyzed. Slated for the trash heap, he and a couple other refuse heroes were saved, at least for a couple years, by my lying, cheating, and stealing.

Another, an elderly man (younger than I am now) known as "Pop," the cook in our camp, was riding his bicycle over a little bridge when a big "lorry" truck crushed him into the bridge wall and mangled his legs. The lorry continued on, of course, unknowing or uncaring, and left Pop in the dirt until some Vespa three-wheeler took pity on him. Pop screamed to be taken to the American camp. That was a wonderful evening. Sergeant Freedman, the team medic, sawed off Pop's legs as I watched, suppressing the gag reflex. Freedman went with "the agency" and was killed in a later war. A much shorter version of Pop lived—but he retired to his hut in the village with his old wife and could no longer walk or work. I "killed," with the Major's connivance, a bunch more strikers; then he and I, and a few other members of the team, went to see Pop a couple times, and I gave him maybe $500. He cried and kissed my hand. I forget how I felt. Not good, as I recall, because I was due to leave this beautiful shit-hole of a country, and he was an old man doomed to stay there, with no legs and no future.

I lied, cheated, and stole money for the paralyzed, pockmarked Sergeant Yao and for poor Pop, but I will belly up to the bar at my last judgment with unknocking knees for breaking the rules of the Army, and the law, for the two of them.

But Calhoun's "line in the sand" was moving toward me. I had other "expenses." The Vietnamese Special Forces Major periodically came to me with his own expenses and asked if I could help him with a certain amount. "Yes, sir, Tu Ta," I would say (usually, but not always). He'd give me a list of imaginary strikers I could "kill" for their death gratuities. Within an hour, I'd have a list of Vietnamese names, and I'd give the Vietnamese major money for his "expenses" (probably bribes and kickbacks to his superiors, along with some stuff for himself). And as Calhoun's line in the sand moved stealthily closer, I diverted a small amount to my own expenses—creature comforts for the not-so-miserable, sandbagged, plywood "team house" the 15 Americans lived in. Actually, it wasn't that bad, and it could have been a lot worse.

Special Forces troopers have a way of making themselves comfortable.

I'd see the Major—my boss, a great multiwounded legend of the Green Berets—and tell him, dryly, "Sir, I had to kill ten more guys today for the money." He would avert his face, laughing, and extend the upward-facing flat of his palm toward me: "Bill, I don't want to hear it! Do what you have to do, but don't tell me."

This book isn't about me. But I'm not writing about behaviors I got off the Internet. I almost signed up for another tour in Nam, but I didn't. I know that if I had, that year might have brought further slips and tumbles down the slippery slope, one of the truest and most visually evocative, if overused, clichés in the media. In another year I probably would have been justifying a new Rolex watch or blue sapphire ring (Special Forces affectations) for the boss and me as I plowed through the line in the sand that would have gotten further and further behind me, my upbringing, and the seventh commandment. I'd heard about other guys who left Vietnam with duffel bags full of U.S. currency gained through black-market deals. Revulsion? Disgust? Outrage? Not really. I probably would never have done it, but the dreamy view of a 23-year-old with $100,000 tax free in 1969 might some day have had some appeal.

One day, I approached Calhoun's line and ran from it like a rabbit. After a firefight with a small North Vietnamese unit, we captured an odd-looking Vietnamese man who was carrying a "base plate" for a Russian or Chinese mortar tube in the area where we had just had the firefight. He had no explanation (through an interpreter) for his behavior. Jittery and wakeful, we had been heavily patrolling the area because of increasing rumors that the enemy was "building ladders" to breach our wire and berm for an attack. An American intelligence officer and I (along with an interpreter) brought the captive into a hut in the camp and began interrogating him. His answers to our questions made no sense, even to the Vietnamese interpreter, judging by his eye rolling and arm gestures. So I slapped the captive around the little hut a few times, unable to hit with a closed fist someone half my size. The intelligence officer obviously felt otherwise: He threw the detainee on a rude table in the hut, inserted his bowie knife into the man's skin and under his breastbone, and began prying upward. As the screams reached human-generated decibels I had never heard before, I began sweating profusely and was enveloped with the feeling of "What the hell am I doing here?" I begged for a stop and then said. "I can't do this." I left the hut, moved quickly back to the team house (followed by the screams), and headed to the barbed-wire camp perimeter (where the screams still haunted me). I wondered again, "What the hell am I doing here?"

Turns out our torture victim was a lunatic, a village idiot who had wandered into the area of the firefight and picked up the "base plate" left by the enemy. Instincts (I don't know, maybe timidity) had at least pulled me back from doing something that today might still be interfering with my usually pleasant dreams.

I wonder what goes through the mind of a young CIA guy as he sets up the water-torture board for the disreputable, wild-eyed possible terrorist in front of him. "Do I listen to the reflexive gagging and screams as I take him to the perceived doorway of death by drowning? Or do I say, 'Screw this,' and walk out the door to let someone else do it?"

The first cancer cell thing consumes me to a minor degree. At what minute, what second, does it start? Bernie Madoff started his investment business almost 50 years ago. This guy is one of the worst sleazes in capitalist history, in terms of knowingly inflicting misery on a large number of people. Probably not from malice, but from reckless greed. He probably didn't start in 1960 with a cranial mission statement that said, "Hey, I think I'll start a Ponzi scheme... maybe screw some friends from a Florida club I may belong to some day. Maybe trash thousands of doctors, nurses, and pension contributors who will trust me to provide for their retirement. Yeah! That's the ticket!" No, he likely ran a reputable fund with a reputable and highly respectable return until he hit a bad year or couple of bad quarters. Then he did a little Ponzi stuff to preserve his track record of returns; then he did some more and enjoyed the billions and the unbelievable lifestyle. And then one morning he woke up to the reality that he was a swindler and sociopath and said, "Hey, screw it. Too late to turn back." A couple suicides later and a couple "clangs" as cell doors slammed behind him, and I wonder if he thinks about the day that "cell" split and that he let it split.

GE's chief tax officer, John Samuels, holds this view on Enron and how it turned into a cannibalistic Frankenstein: "If you get near [Calhoun's] line, your head can say it's right, although your heart knows it is wrong. Listen to your heart." Samuels says the type of rot that brought Enron down "does not happen frequently at the higher levels of American business."

Albert Jay Nock has posed the question, "How does one know when one is entering a dark age?" It seems that you must calibrate your moral compass to the point that it tells you clearly that a dark age of corroding integrity looms before you. And there is seldom an escape once you enter it.

The Bedroom Counts

Cheating can take many forms. George Jamison says there's no escape from its consequences. Cheating will catch up with you and become your undoing—and that includes marital infidelity. Jamison, as a headhunter, knows more about this than I do. I agree that if a man or woman will break a solemn vow, he or she will not stop for a second to break an SEC rule or break the law outright. But it may not *inevitably* catch up with him, as Jamison asserts. I've seen too many guys in senior positions cheat serially and retire unscathed to rich, even revered retirements.

The integrity standards of an organization come from the top. At every level, management sets the tone with appropriately strident "One strike and you're out" threats, as well as public, gory hangings of malefactors.

The leadership of Enron is now either pushing up daisies or punching out license plates, but those leaders created an atmosphere so toxic that 25-year-olds were baptized in it from the day they walked into the company, with 28-year-old "Masters of the Universe" wannabees deliberately browning out areas of California to create shortages and manipulate energy prices. They laughed, with a cynicism appropriate to 60-year-old sleazebags, as they spent their days in a toilet of cheating, piracy, deception, lies, and filth that cascaded down from and was rewarded by the leadership. The BMWs got bigger, and their souls smaller.

C. S. Lewis, a great Catholic writer, talked about another level of "size matters" in regard to souls. The late Joseph Sobran, who has been called the best political and social columnist of the last 30 years, commented on Lewis's take on *The Screwtape Letters* in "Screwtape Proposes a Toast." And I summarize here: The old devil (that's who Screwtape is, Satan) apologizes to his peers for the "insipid fare of human souls—or such residual puddles of what *once* was soul" on which they are currently feasting. "Oh, to get one's teeth again into...a Henry VIII, or even a Hitler! There was real crackling there; a rage; an egotism, a cruelty only just less robust than our own [the devils']".

Bill Woodburn on Skilling and Enron

Bill Woodburn, a former GE senior executive who was head of several of the most modern and promising businesses, and is now founder of an enormous global infrastructure fund, disabused me of my totally negative view of Skilling.

Woodburn knew Skilling for a long time and considered him a "wonderful guy with absolute integrity." I've quoted Skilling protesting to a woman author who could not figure out the "black box" that was Enron, saying that he was not an accountant and could not explain it, and that she should talk to his chief financial officer.

Woodburn said this was nonsense: "Skilling knew more about accounting than the accountants who worked for him," he said. In fact, Woodburn and Skilling had gone together to a meeting with some senior people of the Federal Regulatory Energy Commission, and by the end of the day (literally, not as a cliché), Skilling knew more about the law than the ones who had briefed them that day. "He had a way of sorting out really important facts, semi-important facts, and irrelevant facts," said Woodburn. His mind operated "like a laser."

"So what happened?" I asked.

"I don't know," he answered "I hadn't seen him in years, and called him up about some college issue about my daughter. We reminisced for a while, but I noticed that, literally every two minutes, he interrupted the conversation to check the Enron stock price. I thought this odd, since I only checked the GE stock price every couple of days." This implied, to Woodburn that Enron was being run for the stock price rather than performance. Sizzle rather than steak.

"So what happened to this guy with 'impeccable integrity'?" I asked. Woodburn said, "I guess he took it to the edge, then way over the edge, and then way, *way* over the edge." It's Calhoun's "line in the sand."

Skilling couldn't get it back. Woodburn's theory was that he wanted to get out. Maybe he prayed that the sham called Enron could plug on for four or five more years, by which time he'd be out of the radioactive zone. But as Woodburn said, "The market slipped, energy prices fell, hedge positions fell apart, and the whole house of cards came crashing down"—secretaries, security guards, cafeteria workers, gardeners, shareowners, and all.

Woodburn was asked to write a letter to the judge before sentencing and did so, asking the judge to "find some way to use that brain to support society." Whether or not it had any effect is not clear. Woodburn thinks that Skilling will be in the can until he's 70.

In any case, the stink and miasma of cheating and dissembling permeated the entire organization at Enron. Auditors Arthur Anderson went down with the ship—or garbage barge—for their winks or eye aversion, too.

Uh, did somebody take the name down from that stadium?

Would your sanctimonious author have acted in exactly the same way if immersed in that culture, as those "kids" in their 20s and early 30s did? Yeah, probably. It was a casino, especially on the trading side. Some of them are probably just fine now, at companies that don't mind inviting in a descented skunk.

I am not proud of the part of my character that would *not* have propelled me out of Enron in a huff of self-righteousness. I probably would have rationalized, a la Calhoun's view, "That's just how they play the game in energy—or whatever." My 26-year-old Army Captain son would have walked out that door—but he's a better man than I am.

At the leadership level, cultivating a culture that develops a grim-faced fanatical bias for integrity while burning with competitiveness and a compulsion to deliver results requires real skill—communications skill, actually. The performance demands must not convey a "head fake" on the role of absolute integrity. Telling a manager, "You get this done, or I'll find some one else who can do it," without reinforcing the basic integrity ground rules can be perceived as a "by any means necessary" statement.

GE bought RCA in 1985, primarily to acquire two of its businesses: NBC, which Jack Welch coveted for its potential and because it would allow him to ameliorate the ho-hum Rust Belt, light bulb company image, and Aerospace, a very good complement to the GE defense businesses. But the business carried with it some troublesome baggage—a recent scandal over "time cards" that put it in the sights of what Welch has called a "government rampage against fraud and abuse."

A culture had developed in this business, which dealt almost exclusively with the government, of charging every nickel that was honestly earned. This was done largely through time cards. The perceived pressure from the top was to bill the government for more and more time, thereby growing earnings. Never, ever was it stated or implied that cheating was permissible. But inevitably, some time cards were falsified to reflect work that had *actually been done* but not charged, so it was inflated into the work of another job. Some moral philosophies call this "occult compensation." A neighbor borrows your tools and, a year later, denies that he has them. You sneak into his garage one night and retrieve them. You are trespassing—maybe breaking and entering—and are now afoul of the law. You have committed an illegal act, but not an immoral one.

In any event, a giant stink enveloped the business, accompanied by fines and government grandstanding. Welch became increasingly uncomfortable with the business he had just acquired, recognizing that a low-level employee at some obscure location had in his hands the power to drag the whole business through the mud—and now, the entire General Electric company. Welch did not like this vulnerability, this taking of GE's destiny—or some part of it—out of its own hands.

The Aerospace business was, like NBC, initially very uncomfortable with its new owner, and Welch and his team went out of their way to welcome them, even taking care of some of the innocents who had been harmed by the government inquisitions, which after all were aimed at protecting taxpayers, as well as advancing some government careers.

GE and Aerospace emerged fairly quickly from government purgatory. But the whole vulnerability issue left an indelible mark in Welch's mind, causing him to despise the ethical minefields that must be traversed in dealing with government contracts, the time cards, and the whole theory of doing business with the government. Aerospace was sold profitably to Lockheed-Martin at the earliest opportunity in the 1990s.

What's your view on this? There were no real bad guys—no crooks—but a business crashed, if it didn't burn. It got in trouble because its leadership failed to emphasize the importance of adhering to the spirit as well as the letter of the law. My view is that the fine, ethical individual—who I knew, who would never have tolerated dishonesty in his business or countenanced the morally neutral alteration of time cards to compensate under the counter for work *actually done* elsewhere or at some other time—should have cultivated a Red Guard fanaticism on the subject. He did not, and many good people paid the price.

You need to be a nut, a monomaniac, a puritan on the subject, to the point of being snickered at nervously and quietly around whatever symbolizes the water cooler today. And if you are fortunate enough to have even a trivial cheater discovered in a violation, however minor, hang him. Hang him high for visibility into the sunlight, like Billy Budd, for all to see. And as the Godfather declared, "Then they would fear you."

If this sounds hysterical, yeah, maybe it is. But consider that you can screw up your operations and get fired. You can get old and in a rut, and crash. You can become irrelevant and burn. Some of these failings are beyond your control. *Integrity is not.* Only you can surrender on this subject. No one can nail you but yourself.

A Paler Shade of Gray: Into the Heart of Ambiguity Without a Compass

This is not a sermonette. Crooks and thieves need to be taken down to the gatehouse at the company, have the stickers shaved off their cars and their passes reclaimed, and be banished. Often crying and unbelievable distress take place at these events. Walking through your office door on a Monday morning to see two grim-faced auditors and a senior security individual greeting you, politely and gravely requesting your laptop, is the stuff of which nightmares are made, particularly if you have a family. You then have to endure the sticker-shaving and gatehouse rituals and go home and tell your children, "Mommy (or Daddy) has decided to leave the company and do something else."

I told my daughter, Regan, who was starting out at NBC Universal, "Put whatever you want down on an expense account, no matter how much of a stretch, but never, *ever* tell a lie." She didn't need this advice and told me so.

Bob Llamas, former head of human resources at Nielsen, told me of a miserable scene in which he had to fire a good woman, a secretary who went out on a legitimate lunch boondoggle with a few other secretaries, ran up a big tab, panicked, inflated the number of people at the "luncheon" and put down names of people who weren't there (who later found out and complained).

Llamas told her that she should have picked up the alcohol, or at least part of it, or volunteered to collect from her colleagues the portion that the eyeshade people would have gagged at. And I have found they don't gag at a lot.

No one I ever heard of was fired for telling the truth on an expense report. They were "nicked," maybe, even for a couple hundred dollars, but not fired. In fact, their superiors and colleagues admired them as truth-tellers.

But let's move up the food chain a bit in the matter of expense accounts. Consider people like Dennis Koslowski, who spent $2 million on a birthday party in Sardinia for his wife, with vodka coming out of the equipment of an ice statue of David. His company picked up half the tab. He'll never pay a price until the business goes to hell—and then the wolves will round them up and send them to jail. And should.

The bottom line is that you can't lie. You can spin and bullshit, to a degree, but *you can't lie.*

Preachy Stuff

I try to avoid preaching, but it's sometimes necessary, in my view. People at all levels of business—and at *any* level of the military—cannot afford any compromise on integrity. You have to be a "church lady," if necessary—a Puritan, a caricature of righteousness. It will come naturally after a while, and it needn't involve posturing as some kind of saint. The "rep" will follow you, keyed to your actions.

The "integrity instinct" is not necessarily instinctual. Here's a quick story to underscore that point.

In the 1980s, GE decided to do what was probably the first stock buyback in the company's history. Welch wanted me to prepare a brochure on what we were doing, so as not to look like we were following a trail of stock "buybackers" who were proliferating at the time because of the frequent pop a buyback achieved on the stock price. The brochure was aimed at disarming the Wall Street voices that might say that this move was just a reflexive shout with the crowd of Fortune 500 companies surfing the rising Dow wave.

So Welch and I worked with the investor relations (IR) guy on the content of our little brochure. I handed it off to the graphics department to put it into an attractive and readable form that the shareowners would actually understand and maybe enjoy. (Okay, that's a stretch.)

I was summoned to Welch's conference room to report on the progress of the brochure. Welch must have been the only CEO in history to be paranoid, schizophrenic, and anal about some freakin' brochure to be issued. But he *understood* nuance and image and knew why this wasn't something to be left to public relations or investor relations alone.

Once again, on being "dragged up" up to the conference room: "So, this looks good so far." (Insert 20 technical comments on unbelievably minute details, like, "Why are you using this funny color?" and "Shouldn't this print be bigger? This is important.") Then I heard the usual, "When are we gonna get a 'final?'"

"Have it for you tomorrow."

The whips and chains were coming out as I prepared to descend to the AV department downstairs. The thing had to look professional, but not too professional. I was trying to leave the lion's den of Welch's office to begin torturing and lashing people in the basement when Welch stopped me. "Bill! Did you tell those guys down there that they absolutely have to keep their mouths shut on this?" (Significant insider trading implications were associated with this information.)

"Yeah, Jack, I did. I told them that anyone who mentioned a word of this to anyone outside of the department would be fired."

I thought that was fairly scary, but not as scary as the rant that followed: "No, not fired—*jail*! Do you understand? *Jail!*"

"Jack, I think I understand."

I went down and, I think, got the point across. But I probably didn't need to. These were a great—and moral—bunch of people.

I have a great and moral Army officer son, but I was troubled by some of the stuff I'd seen on the Internet about Iraq and had seen for myself in Vietnam. As the lieutenant prepared to deploy with his unit to Iraq, I sat with him one afternoon. We shot the breeze, and then I abruptly veered into what was on my mind: "Bill, don't hurt civilians. Don't wipe out an apartment building because a few sniper rounds may have come from there. There are women and children and old people in those buildings. Keep that in mind."

He's is a great and moral kid and a wonderful son, but he unloaded on me after that sermon: "Dad, why do you think you need to tell me all that? Don't you think I know that?" He was indignant and angry. But I have no regrets.

I remember the childish saying we used to parrot at Airborne and Special Forces training: "Kill 'em all and let God sort them out."

No, God will sort *you* out if you do that.

My Bill didn't need me to give him advice. He has his own moral compass—a reasoned, moral, and beautiful one. But I just wanted to make sure the compass was calibrated.

Be a Puritan. Beat yourself up on the easy moral decisions— expense account stuff, time card fraud, procedures that screw clients by "churning," and the like.

The more nuanced questions are tougher—much tougher.

Was the sermon on stealing or insider trading, too obvious? Let's move into murkier waters.

An Even Paler Shade of Gray

"Bang, clang, bang." A senior staff member was assigned temporarily to a major GE location, a manufacturer of large steam turbine generators. On his first day there, he saw a few of these behemoth contraptions being loaded on to flatbed trucks. They departed. Next morning, the clanging began. It was audible from headquarters! "What the hell is that?" Workmen across the street were putting the finishing touches on these multimillion-dollar machines, one or two of which could power a small city. Why were they doing this across the street?

The business wanted to book the sales before the quarter closed. The turbines were sold, almost ready to ship to the customer, but the SEC regulation stated that they had to be "removed from the property" before the earnings could be booked.

Lloyd Trotter, the recently retired vice chairman of GE, told me, "Customers have to take full title on the product (not including warrantee claims)."

Is there a moral dimension here? I don't think so. Certainly nothing should cause you to toss and turn at night. You're playing the game by the defined ground rules.

What does the government think? It's fairly noncommittal but is poised to strike at any moment if career advancement is seen as an option for prosecuting and securing a big scalp for some 30-something lawyer's belt.

But what should you be thinking about the banging and clanging across the street? Is Calhoun's "line in the sand" moving toward you? I don't know. But you need to talk to people as you push forward. Corporate leaders and the shareowners want those earnings. Do you refuse? Do you get up on your high horse and strike a blow for purity and evolving puritanical SEC standards and regulations? Go ahead. You can probably get a job as the CFO of the local Salvation Army Battalion, but that's about it.

Some of these regulations are totally stupid and deserve to be ignored, but they are a nest of cobras sunning themselves on the side of your career road and waiting to put a couple of fang marks in your career's ass.

Keep aware that there are snakes out there—the government and lawyers, to repeat myself. The advice of Jim McNerney, of Boeing (coming soon in these pages), is crucial here: Make everyone of importance to your function and your life a partner and a confidant. Have them call you if something smells funny or if they have to make a decision that could involve the feds. Once again, we are not talking about blatantly illegal behavior.

I wish I had more of a contribution to make to the understanding of integrity. You simply have to carefully build your own compass and then steer by it. A "clang, clang" across the street as the workers finish your product so that it will comply with SEC bureaucrats' arbitrary regulations is not, in my view, a bad thing. But it can *become* a bad thing if some ambitious lawyer decides to go elephant hunting and you're the one whose tusks are sticking out of the company face and fall in the crosshairs of the 600 Nitro Express.

Work on that compass. Incorporate the overused but useful "sniff test" and the notion of going home to look into the eyes of your spouse and talk about what you did—or are thinking of doing or are being asked or advised to do. And if you get the "fish-eye," rethink it.

Or consider this better view: John Samuels, who is the "general in charge" of the massive army of GE tax people, told me an excellent way to stay out of trouble with the feds: "In my area [tax] we always imagine and pretend that we work for the government, and thinking from that perspective, if we would not agree with whatever we might be planning, we simply don't do it."

Never Lie: Part 83

A point I beat to death in my few written lectures to the Jack Welch MBA candidates is that you can put down the most outrageous stuff on your expense account, as long as it's the truth.

> State the purpose of the event: "We had a great meeting and went out to celebrate with the team, which had worked like dogs for two weeks to make this a success. Dinner was over $4,000, and we had some champagne (Dom Perignon). Some customers came along from Amalgamated, and we brought them into the celebration and took them along afterward for some entertainment, including lap dances.
>
> Receipts are attached.

You will probably—or maybe—get whacked by the auditors (depending on your rank) for a few hundred bucks or more, and you can assess your team for the majority of the total. Let them know before the festivities begin that this is a possibility. Customers get a free ride, so to speak.

You will *not* be accused of being a liar—because you have *not* lied. You may have a follow-up discussion with your spouse over the lap dance issue, but that's a different story.

Nothing's worse than a liar. Most people in organizations generally shy away from arrogant bastards, weirdos, flakes, lunatics, and the like, but *liars* of any degree—proven liars even in one "small matter"—are detested lepers. In the military, they are *worse* than detested. At West Point, they are instantly thrown out. Pants on fire. Kicked in the pants—and kicked quite far.

Truth telling, even when it hurts, is absolutely the number one totem you must worship in your business or institutional life—or your marriage, for that matter.

And the terrible part about lying is that it is indelible: You cannot get your honesty or your reputation back.

I recall being told this by a very senior officer of GE a long time ago about another officer: "He's a goddamned liar and a sleazebag—and the fact that he is an officer in the General Electric Company makes me sick."

He wasn't around for long, and to be fair, I don't know what he did to merit this tirade. But the horse collar was upon him.

Welch and everyone else I worked for at GE were subjected to furious vituperation and criticism for being monsters, town destroyers, bloated capitalists, and worse. But I never heard the word *liar* used to describe any one of them. An accusation like that would have prompted a call to "say exactly what you mean—to what do you refer?" And there would have been no answer.

But What If You're in Marketing?

This is a tough case, because the accepted rules of the game are predicated on the widely understood assumption that marketing is basically the trumpeting of exaggerated claims and stories. The customers, unless credulous or just stupid, know this to be true and typically sift through the pile of horse crap to find the pony or two that might justify their purchase.

This is typically a lower-level consumer-related scam.

At higher levels, it is much rarer, because if you sell a customer some jet engines or locomotives that don't perform according to your claims, you can kiss those customers—and probably the whole industry—goodbye. Large-scale marketing fraud is rare. The Bernie Madoff affair is only partly marketing; it largely falls into the realm of outright fraud.

But it does exist.

And has existed for millennia. Allow me to burnish my nonexistent classical credentials with an example from Cicero, the most famous of Roman orators. My son, who *does* have classical credentials, supplied me with this reference while we discussed the subject of marketing and integrity on Skype a few months ago when he was in Iraq.

This from Cicero's *De Officiis*:

> Suppose again that an honest man is offering a house for sale on account of certain undesirable features of which he himself is aware but which nobody else knows; suppose it is unsanitary, but has the reputation of being healthful; suppose it is not generally known that vermin are to be found in all the bedrooms; suppose, finally, that it is built of unsound timber and likely to collapse, but that no one knows about it except the owner; if the vendor does not tell the purchaser these facts but sells him the house for far more than he could reasonably have expected to get for it, I ask whether his transaction is unjust or dishonorable.
>
> "Yes," says Antipater, "it is; for to allow a purchaser to be hasty in closing a deal and through mistake, is worse than refusing to set a man on his way: It is deliberately leading a man astray."

"Can you say," answers Diogenes, "that he compelled you to purchase, when he did not even advise it? He advertised for sale what he did not like; you bought what you did like. If people are not considered guilty of swindling when they place upon their placards FOR SALE: A FINE VILLA, WELL BUILT, even when it is neither good nor properly built, still less guilty are they who say nothing in praise of their house. For there the purchaser may exercise his own judgment, what fraud can there be on the part of the vendor? But if, again, not all that is expressly stated has to be made good, do you think a man is bound to make good what has not been said? What, pray, would be more stupid than for a vendor to recount all the faults in the article he is offering for sale? And what would be so absurd as for an auctioneer to cry, at the owner's bidding, "Here is an unsanitary house for sale'?"

The fact is that merely holding one's peace about a thing does not constitute concealment, but concealment consists in trying for your own profit to keep others from finding out something that you know, when it is for their interest to know it. And who fails to discern what manner of concealment that is and what sort of person would be guilty of it? At all events he would be no candid or sincere or straightforward or upright or honest man, but rather one who is shifty, sly, artful, shrewd, underhand, cunning, one grown old in fraud and subtlety. Is it not inexpedient to subject oneself to all these terms of reproach and many more besides?

If, then, they are to be blamed who suppress the truth, what are we to think of those who actually state what is false? Gaius Canius, a Roman knight, a man of considerable wit and literary culture, once went to Syracuse for a vacation, as he himself used to say, and not for business. He gave out that he had a mind to purchase a little country seat, where he could invite his friends and enjoy himself, uninterrupted by troublesome visitors. When this fact was spread abroad, one Pythius, a banker of Syracuse, informed him that he had such an estate; that it was not for sale, however, but Canius might make himself at home there, if he pleased; and at the same time he invited him to the estate to dinner next day. Canius accepted. Then Pythius, who, as might be expected of a moneylender, could command favors of all classes, called the fishermen together and asked them to do their fishing the next day out in front of his villa, and told them what he wished them to do. Canius came to dinner as a fleet of boats sailed before their eyes; each fisherman brought in, in turn, the catch that he had made; and the fishes were deposited at the feet of Pythius.

"Pray, Pythius," said Canius thereupon, "what does this mean?—all these fish—all these boats?"

"No wonder," answered Pythius; "this is where all the fish in Syracuse are; here is where the fresh water comes from; the fishermen cannot get along without this estate."

Inflamed with desire for it, Canius insisted upon Pythius's selling it to him. At first he demurred. To make a long story short, Canius gained his point. The man was rich, and, in his desire to own the country seat, he paid for it all that Pythius asked; and he bought the entire equipment, too. Pythius entered the amount upon his ledger and completed the transfer.

The next day Canius invited his friends; he came early himself. Not so much as a boat was in sight. He asked his next-door neighbor whether it was a fishermen's holiday, for not a sign of them did he see.

"Not so far as I know," said he; "but none are in the habit of fishing here. And so I could not make out what was the matter yesterday."

Canius was furious.

Apparently, 2,000 years ago, lawyers had not yet been invented. (I wonder if the expression "There's something fishy about this deal" came from this story? Sorry, I'll get even fishier in a minute.)

This differs substantially, in my view, from the claims of the makers of those blade-razors who tout the effectiveness of a buzzing noise while you are shaving. Seems like it doesn't do anything, as has been alleged and not really contested.

There are claims that buzzing makes your face smoother. Fine. That's marketing, not lying.

But *liar* is a word that should never be said of you or anyone with whom you associate in business, in the military, in marriage—anywhere!

Slouching Further into the Gray Zone

As I've said before, I am on the faculty of the Jack Welch Management Institute, a testimony to the intellectual resilience of the man for whom it is named. Welch did not speak to me for two years because of my last book, *Jacked Up*. But he specified that I do the communications and ethics lectures for his MBA program. (Paid, of course—not as much as I would like, but as a gesture of respect, if not affection, from someone whom I consider an old friend and certainly a benefactor.) In one of the lectures, I tried to show some further gradients of "grayness" in integrity that can cause you to crash, burn, and lose.

Let me describe a case that we pose to the MBA candidates in the program, and then we'll move on. I hand-wrote on my printed copy of this lecture, "May be preachy." That was not my intent. In fact, I admit that we don't know the answers to some of these integrity questions, once we get behind the obvious "Don't cheat on your expense account stuff" and, above all, "Never lie."

You are close to closing a major deal in Russia. Near the close, the subject of "agents' fees" comes up—relatively minor amounts, in the context of the deal. You know what we are talking about here: bribes. You also know that your competitors (some not encumbered by company rules about paying foreign bribes, some from countries where they are not even frowned upon) are lining up with cash in hand. Your company will lose the deal if you don't do likewise. It's simply a way of doing business in some countries, so you grease the people, win the deal, and return home a hero. Is what you did moral? Probably. There's no real moral dimension here, although it is contrary to U.S. law and the rules of the best companies.

That "hero's welcome" at America's best companies today will be you getting fired.

Brackett Denniston, General Counsel at GE, spoke to us in February 2012 at a small GE luncheon and made this point on the subject: "If you are in India, or China, or Russia (which is still as crooked as a dog's hind leg) on a locomotive deal and the person you are dealing with announces that he or she would like to visit, in addition to the locomotive headquarters in Erie, Pennsylvania, New York City and Disneyworld, *that's a bribe*. If you pay for it, you are *fired*."

People come to GE and say, "We know you don't bribe. And that's fine." In my view, for what it's worth, bribing in international business does not have a moral dimension, especially when dealing with corrupt but *nouveau riche* foreign countries. I cannot imagine, as a Catholic, going to confession and saying in the quiet darkness of the confessional, "Bless me, Father, for I have sinned. I brought a client over on the locomotive deal and sent him and one of his daughters to Disneyworld." There would be either silence or choked laughter from behind the screen.

Now, taking a customer out to dinner with several bottles of Dom Perignon and some other items of "grease" (I got some golf travel bags) is fine. Grease, within limits, can be a good thing, at least for the "greasee." When I would visit a company to prepare a speech for someone at GE Headquarters, I would be taken to dinner by one of their senior people. Before I could order a martini, my host would say, "First, some grease," and produce, as I said, a good golf bag with the business logo on it and some other really nice items. No junk. I used to love to travel to speeches with Larry Bossidy when he was vice chairman (later he became CEO of Honeywell) because the hosting companies or businesses would give him some really neat gifts, such as a beautifully framed print that I would look at and possibly compliment if I liked it on the way back to the helicopter. Typically, Larry would say, "You want it? I've got this stuff all over the house." He didn't have to ask twice.

Contrast this environment with the one I encountered while working at the Pentagon. I accompanied Norm Augustine, then Undersecretary of the Army and a three-star Army General, to the headquarters of a company (Westinghouse, I believe) that was working on some kind of radar we were buying. The briefings were delivered during a working luncheon, and the luncheon consisted of a chicken sandwich, a pickle, and some fruit, washed down with some cans of warm 7UP. When the luncheon concluded, I had to hit up the Secretary and the General and myself for a dollar apiece to pay for it, and I handed over the money to one of the company people. I laughed about it on the way back to the Pentagon, over the whine and "blade flap" of the Vietnam-era Huey, and was told, "Are you kidding? How'd you like a newspaper article or TV piece under the headline, 'Pentagon Brass Dined and Feted at Contractor Doing Millions in Radar Work'? I'd rather pay the buck for that shit sandwich. Besides, it's in the regs. You can't take anything."

When in Rome, find out the "regs" and comply with them.

If your company plays internationally and has no provisions about paying bribes, go ahead (unless it's against extant laws). No high-horses here. But increasingly, big American companies are making it a career destroyer—and a trap for losers. Come back from a lost contract caused by failure to pay a bribe and tell your bosses or your board what happened; if they chew you out, leave and tell a more scrupulous prospective employer what happened.

"Situational ethics" is a morally bankrupt term meaning essentially doing morally right or wrong things based on the needs of winning and competing. I add another construction: "situational compliance," which includes driving the locomotives across the street to be finished (on rails, of course) so you can book the sales. This is cynical compliance with a stupid government regulation and has no moral dimension. Thomas More, while refusing to disobey his conscience and publicly approve of Henry VIII's marriage and disobedience to the Pope, nevertheless searched for every way to *approve* the oath of loyalty to the king, so as to keep his soul and his head. In the end, he kept only the former. Oddly, company policy is often more restrictive than the law. Have fun!

If you are new to an institution and unfamiliar with its practices, *ask* before you do anything that might be in the gray zone. That may be covering your ass (CYA), but one's ass needs to be covered in this sniper-infested business, government, and political climate.

Mark Vachon, a GE vice president, formerly of the medical systems business and now head of the company's giant "Ecomagination" initiative, has a view on failure. He told me that failing because of cheating, lying, or breaking the law is more than merely embarrassing. Here's his view: "Fail in a *lofty* dimension—you swung too hard, or too fast, or reached too far for the ball." In doing so, you may walk back to the dugout disappointed, but with your head held high and with probably more "at-bats" in front of you. (Carly Fiorina comes to mind.) Cheat, lie, or otherwise break the rules and get caught, and you walk away with soiled uniform pants and no respect from anyone—and with your team and your company very possibly in ruins. That trivial time card violation at GE's future Aerospace business in the 1980s put a little cloud over the entire company and was one of the major reasons—if not *the* major reason—Welch got rid of this multibillion-dollar business. It had *shamed us.*

A Bridge—or Causeway—Too Far

Bob Nelson, a former vice president at GE and still Welch's trusted financial analyst, told me he read and completely believes this: The system tests you one level or more beyond your capabilities (if those capabilities are at all limited—and in some people they are not). The promotional peristalsis that pushes people through the intestines of all large companies—and other institutions—will push some obviously bright and talented, and so-far successful, people to "X" (your true capability level), or maybe to "X + 2," or higher—sometimes very much higher.

This is a Peter Principle derivative.

As the sainted Michael Jackson observed, you need to "look at the man [or woman] in the mirror." You have to know yourself. And you have to realize, as Clint Eastwood observed in one of the *Dirty Harry* movies, "A man's got to know his limitations."

Nelson told me that his job as Welch's financial analyst was what he was good at: "I would not have been a good CFO." But "overpromotion," the incubus that haunts the dreams of young executives (yeah, right), is common and even rampant in large institutions. Its victims—for, paradoxically, that's what they are—need to recognize that, at least for the present, they are in over their heads. Failure to grasp that reality leads them finding themselves, like Wiley Coyote, chasing not a roadrunner, but a huge career, and running off a cliff, visibly spinning their legs for a brief and dramatic time before crashing and burning—and being removed.

Nelson claims that "staff people" (human resources, finance, and marketing people, for example) are more likely to succeed than "line people" (operations people) because, as he says with his characteristic reticence, those in line operations often have "visions of grandeur" and react to potential failure in their new responsibilities with arrogance and a refusal to reach out and learn and trust. Steve Bennet, former CEO of Intuit (Turbotax), told me, "They often tend to focus on managing their 'image,' convince themselves that they really are great, and do all sorts of things to facilitate that image, surrounding themselves with lower-performing players who kiss their asses. Then they become more and more insulated from the real workings of the organization."

Talk about a formula for organizational suicide! Hire the competence-challenged. They make *you* look better!

A few companies have CEOs, boards, or HR directors who are smart enough to pick up these behaviors and act to correct them. But not all do.

Welch's performance in removing those wobbling nervously or arrogantly across the bridge too far above their capabilities, or throwing up over the railing, was spotty. He could be temporarily blinded by a form of corporate love for his creations—and, after a decade, they were almost *all* his creations. But he had the intellectual capacity and courage to do what had to be done when reality sat on his desk for a while and poked him, as my Golden Retriever does to me when it's time to eat or be let out.

One guy—and a very big player he was, and someone I actually liked—who was running one of GE's biggest businesses had a view of himself as "above the fray" of actual operations, according to Nelson (who knew more about the man's business than he did). The man was a Brit; with their mellifluous tones and graceful demeanor, Brits often appear more intelligent and capable than they may be, even to someone like Welch. An Irish anglophile with an IQ higher than anyone I have ever met, Welch was entranced by anyone with that admittedly charming accent, especially when contrasted with his nasal, whining Boston argot or my crude but fading Brooklynese.

Nelson and I (along with several other observers) would tell Welch of this man's "regal" behavior, and he would listen and process the data, albeit with resistant body language. This man's demeanor and attitude violated several of the GE values that we were relentlessly reminding our employees to adopt and follow. He found customers a boring nuisance and considered employees rabble to be exploited and then discarded when convenient.

On one occasion in his new kingdom, he had the facility engineers expand the lines on his parking space so that none of the *lumpenproles* would clumsily swing open a door and scratch his top-of-the-line BMW or one of his Ferraris. The hourly people, who despised him, began bringing birdseed to work, and stealthily throwing handfuls on the Beemer as they walked by, attracting the winged denizens of the facility lot to alight upon and crap on his cars. On another occasion, he deigned to allow the annoying customers (who provided billions in revenue) to attend a reception at his palatial house, but had movie-theatre-style velvet ropes installed in front of the stairway so that none of the scum would be allowed to enter the sanctum above.

On one occasion, I recounted to Welch the humiliation this person had visited on a friend senior to me by having my friend phone the guy's wife and debase himself in apology for having "disturbed" her at home with a business call for His Highness. Welch told me that he had made a call to verify the account I had related and understood, "It was as you said."

He had an unhappy and worried look on his face.

The clock was ticking.

It continued to tick for this guy, who, as Nelson put it, was "phenomenal at disguising his lack of involvement in the business."

This guy would stand up at financial analyst meetings in New York that I helped run and tell the audience, "This year *I'm* going to defeat Siemens (or Brown-Boveri, or somebody) in this market segment or that." And then he'd announce his intention to "defeat" all the competing CEOs and then name the ones *he* was going to *crush* or *smash*, or whatever.

He asked me once, when he had completed one of his arrogant performances, how I thought he had done. After I tore my eyes away from his $10,000-dollar suit and gold Rolex the size of an alarm clock that must have cost five times the suit, I told him, "You were fine." (He had a B+ presence and style, hugely enhanced by the accent.) "Except for two things: One, you never use 'I' in an analyst pitch. This is a 'We' company. And, two, analysts hate it when you trash or rhetorically shake your fists at competitors in presentations made to them."

I might have mentioned the Godfather's advice from the Puzo book: "Never threaten."

He looked at me for a moment and said, "Well, that's good input." Then he turned on the heels of his thousand-dollar shoes (I may be selling him short on the shoes) and walked away to speak to more important folks. There were tons of them in the room.

He later crashed, of course, when Welch could not avoid the inescapable conclusion, signaled by a flashing sign on a mounting pile of evidence that this particular emperor was missing a few garments.

More amusing data on this case comes later. This individual, serially personable and bright, should have been in formalin at the Peter Principle Museum for egregious overpromotion and inability, or unwillingness to recognize and cope with it.

The question I posed to Bob Nelson of GE and both Kip Condron and Andrew McMahon of Axa-Eqitable was this: "Say I get tapped for a much bigger job than I think I am capable of handling at this point in my development. What should I do? Turn it down?" ("Sorry, sir, I'd really like to be a vice president, or division manager, or battalion commander, or head nurse, or whatever, but I think I'm not ready for it, and you should probably pick somebody else. In fact, I think Jim, Suzy, or Trish would be better candidates. But thanks for asking. I'm honored.")

Realistic?

I have to quote Steve Martin on this one: "Naaahh!"

So we pretty much agree, I would guess, that although really perceptive, wise, and savvy people would avoid campaigning for jobs they sense—or know—are beyond their capabilities, most of us would not turn them down, if bestowed. I haven't. But then again, I haven't been "bestowed upon" that often in my modest career.

But enough about me. How do you get that big "bestowal" you've been angling for? Some views follow.

Landing That Big Job for Which You May Not Be Qualified: Sorry, Babe, You Don't Really Look That Good in That Red Sox Uniform

Andrew McMahon of Axa-Equitable, who looks like a ballplayer (or, at least, a "player") and is chairman of Axa Financial U.S., claims that the first thing baseball scouts ask themselves when looking at a prospect is, "Does he *look* like a ballplayer?" Crazy formulation, and one that would have eliminated George Herman Ruth's fat, sloppy carcass from consideration but would have guaranteed Mantle, Reggie, or Paul McNeill a shot.

Kip Condron, Andrew McMahon's boss and president of AXA, agrees. He told me of a senior guy in his industry who had "been around" and done pretty well but unexpectedly got put "on the market."

Said Condron, "The guy [turned] out to be a zero—maybe not a zero, but certainly not the big number he was up for." The man didn't get the job after several interviews that degenerated into painful, vapid, pro-forma persiflage. One of the interviewers in the chain commented to Condron, "He's no good, but, boy, can he wear a suit."

Condron's response, with endearing honesty and modesty: "I'm not great looking, but I'm okay. I always bought great suits. I couldn't afford to look bad."

I'm not sure any of us can afford to "look bad," although, as the years move along, the mirror tells me I may be working on it.

Learn How to Wear That Suit

If you're up for a lab or IT job and you look like a disheveled swine, it probably won't hurt you. Would you have hired Einstein for a management-level job in PR or finance?

I didn't think so.

Condron told me of another senior manager he hired from one of his field offices to be manager of sales for the whole company. This guy looked great, interviewed well, and got the job. Off they went to one of these usually inane several-day conferences in which the attendees usually undertook a Meyers-Briggs psychometric assessment.

The new manager of sales, so recently hired, turned out to be an *introvert* and acted like one for the short time he had the job. How does one get to be promoted to the (X+1)—or, in this case, X+4 or 5—before crashing and burning? How does an introvert get promoted to national sales manager? Andrew McMahon jumped into the conversation at this point to quote the endlessly wise and amusing Warren Buffet, with the observation, "Sometimes the best performance you will get from someone will be in the interview."

One way to be put on the train-wreck track is to be fortunate (or unfortunate) enough to work for a succession of passive managers along your career path who will promote you to get you out of their hair, much as do miserable public school teachers who pass morons and sociopaths along to the next grade to get them out of their classroom and into some other victim's classroom.

I have seen near-violent confrontations in faculty lounges over the "pass the trash" issue. I resisted doing so when I taught junior high English in Puerto Rico long ago and gave in only once, to a nice eighth-grade kid whose English was a few points below passing. His mother was dying of cancer, and I agonized with my best friend (also on the faculty) about failing this kid for the year. I continued to cite my rules and principles, until he came up to me in the faculty room as grades were to be turned in and said, "None of my business, but if you fail this kid, you're a prick." I passed him— he wasn't trash—and it has never kept me awake at night.

Good senior business leaders will hold to account those who engage in passive behavior, because it can kill a company if widespread. Part of being an effective leader is coming down to someone's door saying, "You got a minute?" and explaining, as gently as candor will permit, "This job is turning out to be a bit over your head (for reasons then enumerated), and I'd like you to begin looking around for something else, either inside the company or outside, let's say, in two months. This isn't working for you or me. Let me know if I can help."

Then leave the poor bastard, with three kids in college, to call his wife and tell her the good news. That's what real leaders have to do: pay with pain and suffering on everyone's part for the cowardice of the *faux* leaders who passed someone along with warm performance reviews over the years. An excuse sometimes offered in their own defense is the reluctance of leaders to write a bad performance review or negative "letter of recommendation," for fear of being sued.

And this excuse is not, by any means, invalid. The lawyers are out there, thrashing around with dorsal fins protruding from the waters, waiting to take the cases of these poor souls who were given

"B" ratings over the years and should have been fired or shunted into smaller jobs, and now have encountered a leader with the courage to write the truth on why this person should be fired.

Then when the poor guy is finally sent home by a true leader, he points to 10 or 20 years of positive, even glowing performance appraisals by other gutless bosses and says, as he calls his lawyer, "Everyone else thought I was great. This guy is the only one with the problem!"

Condron and McMahon's consensus was that "fear of failure" on the part of people in leadership positions is okay as long as it doesn't lead to an aversion to making big decisions that might lead to failure. During the Civil War, George McClellan was paralyzed by fear of defeat and had to be removed from command by Lincoln, who was exasperated by his dawdling and conservatism. Eisenhower, nearly a century later, was clearly daunted by the fear that the Normandy invasion might fail and result in crushing defeat for the Allies. He even had a note prepared and in his pocket telling the Allied commanders and president of the disaster—maybe they'd be thrown back into the water, with the attendant enormous casualties and maimed men, abandoned and writhing, then bleeding to death or drowning, as the remaining ships pulled out of sight.

But then, in the face of marginal weather, he girded his loins, so to speak, and said, "Go."

On a much more mundane level, the mess that rocked NBC late-night programming recently—you know, Conan and Jay—was the result of a calculated gamble, and it failed. But management cannot be faulted for decisiveness and making some decisions that had to be made. Entertainment is weird, a different kettle.

In a remarkably frank and fearless conversation, Condron and McMahon threw out a few observations on how candidates potentially slated for bigger jobs lose it—like, by being fat. Fat? Yeah, you heard it. Fat guys don't fare well in interviews. Why? According to Condron and McMahon, being way overweight implies weakness and lack of self-discipline. For men as well as women? No, at least not in my observation—and I couldn't get anyone to touch this with the proverbial 10-footer.

Bennett, former chairman of Intuit, sees that "people who look great [as Steve does] manage well upward." At the same time, many of them also begin to "kick downward." Steve says they often "get the big jobs" but don't have the talent or experience to succeed in them. Again, it's the Peter Principle.

Some Views on Coping or Crashing When the Big Job You're Not Ready for Falls in Your Lap

I posed the following question to Andrew McMahon, Kip Condron, Jim McNerney, Steve Bennett, Dave Calhoun, and others: "C'mon, what am I supposed to tell people who get a Peter Principle promotion and know they're not ready for the job? Don't take it?"

Imagine that: "I'm sorry—I'd like to be vice president and general manager of that division, but I've thought about it, and it's beyond my experience and capabilities. And as someone once said, 'The higher a monkey climbs up a tree, the more you can see of his (or her) ass.' But thanks for the offer. I'm honored."

Yeah, right. That'll happen.

McNerney, of Boeing, claims it need not happen. Take that promotion, move into that big job, and succeed in it! After all, he did that all the way up to the big chair at Boeing: "I've been given promotions—big new jobs—typically after my predecessor had been relieved [fired] after failing to solve big problems, and I wake up on day one and ask myself, 'Okay, what the hell do I do now, moving into not only a totally new environment, but a troubled, toxic one, as well?' And the answer that has always worked for me is to find the answers from other people. Gather the smart people around you, confide in them, be frank with them about your weaknesses, ask for their help, and make them your confidants. At first, all the important answers will lie outside of you, but you must find them quickly. If your family was sick or threatened, you would act immediately and do whatever you had to do to get help. And talking to ass-kissers is like talking to yourself—crazy and useless.

"You don't have to walk around like John the Baptist, abasing yourself and wailing. Just let your new 'best friends' (because that's what they *must become*) know that you are intensely ambitious and desirous of succeeding and that you need them to help you do so. If they help you, advise you, and stick with you, you will take them with you and make them wealthy and successful. If they ever lie to you or kiss your ass (without cause), you will get rid of them and leave them behind."

Should make for a fun bunch of meetings—or maybe just a *few* meetings, after you have separated in your mind the eagles from the turkeys.

Mark Vachon, in his GE business CEO roles, had a routine: He befriended his HR guy (or woman) and his CFO, which he called his "Triangle Club." He listened to them on a daily basis—really listened. And then he periodically convened off-site what he called his "Breakfast Club," to tell him what his "blind spots" were.

Vachon further relied on friends ("wingmen," as some people call them). These are the people who are not even in the same business or same company, but are smart and incisive, and who will tell you as you are teeing up the ball on a Saturday morning that you are dead wrong, or going in the wrong direction, or even "full of shit" in what you are doing. And this is with no interest in currying favor, no interest in the rewards of your success—they're just good friends who like you and want to see you succeed.

Vachon and I were amazed at how Welch solicited our opinions. Vachon was a junior superstar, and I was a speechwriter nobody;

we were brain-drained by the world's business superstar. Opinions are free from friends, subordinates, and colleagues, and you're not required to go with them. Welch didn't. I could see in his face whether he was valuing what I was saying or hitting the Delete button (never rudely). If you automatically disregard free advice from people who you know are smart, you may be throwing away what occasionally is a treasure. Vachon still marvels at how Welch would listen hungrily to what he said—and not just on the issues related to his function at the time as chief of investor relations.

Vachon's view was, "Someone who is that aware of his weaknesses will not fail." That could probably be argued. But if he or she does fail, it will be with honor and likely second chances.

Steve Bennett says that candidates for losing it often have a significant negative event in their new positions and then typically surround themselves with lower-performing individuals who kiss their asses. They react in exactly the wrong way, by not reaching out for help and counsel, but by instead isolating themselves further from the organization and the people they should be embracing.

Del Williamson, a GE vice president who sold turbines and other high-dollar equipment to electrical utilities for years, described a typical dynamic of the utility industry and too-frequent leadership responses to those dynamics: "The utility is very cyclical, with alternating fat and lean years. If the lean years get too lean, they bring a new CEO in, typically unfamiliar with everything. His response to the crisis is, too frequently, to freeze out the old team, using the rationale that 'I'm going to have to get rid of them anyway.'" Things get worse, as the doomed team smirks from circled wagons, mumbles to each other over cocktails, and talks to headhunters—and even to customers it took the company years to cultivate—about job opportunities.

And what about the new boss of the division or the company? "Screw him. He hates us. And I'm out of here anyway."

Bennett says that leaders who "don't make their teams part of the decision-making process and don't empower people are doomed, and often they bring the entire organization down with them if they are not removed quickly."

These "doomed managers"—and they can be at virtually any level of leadership, from "component" to CEO—often employ what he calls "the hub-and-spoke management system." They deliberately surround themselves with "weaker players who are mere implementers." He says, "They, themselves, do all the 'thinking' because of their arrogance, and delegate 'execution' and make 'gofers' out of people who should be teammates, confidants, advisors, and friends."

According to McNerney, the key is a phrase he no doubt picked up from his military customers: "situational awareness," meaning, "Do a very real assessment of the situation—reaching out for data to your allies, confidants, teammates, and customers—and do it fast!"

I had a friendly $200-an-hour argument with a psychiatrist a few years ago about whether cats are smarter than dogs. I had always believed they were so—most kids are told they are, and they believe it, associating arrogance and aloofness with intelligence.

The shrink said, "No, dogs are smarter than cats. But cats sometimes appear smarter because they are more aware of their environment." The slobbering, panting, banjo-eyed Golden Retriever may not appear to be that bright, compared to the frigid, selfish, quiet, or quietly purring cat—but he or she is smarter, at least, according to the shrink. Full disclosure: I was sent to the shrink to see if he could remedy a type-A personality, so as to minimize a blood pressure situation that threatened to blow my head off. After three or four conversations about animal behavior and golf swings (he is a *plus*-3 handicap pro tour–level player), he gave me some pills and told me to go away. I didn't take them.

But it would appear that a good course of action might be to do what the cats do: Assess your environment, and (the more difficult part) do a cold-blooded assessment of yourself and how your capabilities match what must be done to fix Bennett's "significant negative event" syndrome in progress. You have to save your organization and yourself.

It comes back again to the venerable Shaw's epiphanous self-appraisal, "Hey, I'm not that good an engineer, and I need to do something else."

At senior levels, the "do something else" is to *get help fast.* And that doesn't necessarily mean bringing in McKinsey.

It is difficult, as Boeing's McNerney says, to "get out of your personality—your clothes." But you must. For years now, you've cruised and then accelerated and cruised again. (Nelson says corporate or organizational life is a series of sequences of starting at the bottom, rising to the top, getting promoted, moving back to the bottom, heading back toward the top, and again and again, if you're lucky.)

You've gotten by, or accelerated, on the basis of raw intelligence, suavity, a couple nifty ideas, good results, inoffensive looks, and a great suit. The baggage that sometimes accumulates with this progress is called arrogance. Understandably using a jet-engine analogy, McNerney of Boeing nails it: "Every flame-out has *arrogance* at its core."

"I Couldn't Have Done It Without My Players"—Manager Casey Stengel, after the Yankees Won the 1958 World Series

It has been my observation over several decades that the best, most successful and survivable leaders at every level do as Jim McNerney has suggested: They surround themselves with the very best people available, trust them, wander down to their offices to shoot the breeze and learn, and pay the good ones as much as they can. When the successes and triumphs come, they then trot out these people, rather than themselves, to take the bows.

Overdo the credit you lavish on these people. The worst (or best) comment that will be made on this is, "Sally is giving the team too much credit for that home run. Most of that thinking and the big decisions were hers."

But "the team" will be unendingly loyal to her for letting the sunlight shine on them while she sat in the background, smiling, and will redouble their efforts to make her a star. The organization understands what happens and why it happens, and it scoffs at empty suits or *poseurs* strutting over triumphs brought about largely by people a layer or two below or those who succeed either by being in the right place or through dumb luck.

Understanding Astrophysics

Vachon says unequivocally that, even in the best organizations, "There is a tendency to attribute great results to a 'star.'"

Great leaders at every level have what he called "a healthy dose of humility" and will ask themselves, even as the accolades and the money pour in from the beaming, purring, *uber*boss, "Do I understand the 'physics' of success in this business? And is this success *sustainable*? Is lending mortgage money to people you know will probably default on it a sustainable success? Is cresting on a wave of a distinctly cyclical business, such as power generation, or on a game that cannot go on forever in a dizzying climb, such as commercial real estate, being honest with yourself?"

I've described before the scene described by George C. Scott in *Patton,* of a Roman triumphal parade and the victorious general in his chariot, driving his prisoners before him as he is showered by flowers from the adoring throngs. As ordered, a slave whispers in his ear, "All glory is fleeting."

It can be fleeting, and it is human and business nature to reward success lavishly and then expect more and more of it sooner rather than later.

Encores of successes *will* be expected; and the chariot cannot simply career along through the diminishing flower petals until the wheels come off. Business plans and predictions need to be revised to face reality, and "upstairs" needs to be educated on the facts of life of the business. Dampen and downplay praise and accolades with but a tenuous connection to reality. I never saw at GE people who ran gangbuster-performing businesses react to fulsome praise and huge bonuses and promotions by stating what is generally obvious to everyone: "Hey, thanks, but we just got lucky and we hit this market at the sweet spot. My team did a great job at not screwing up our good luck and maximizing the opportunities that presented themselves to us." Mentioning five or ten of them in your brief remarks will send them home with hearts singing and saying to say to their spouses, "Look honey, look what Barbara said about me today—and she told me later that there would be a bit of a 'hit' on the bonus this year. Let's go to dinner and celebrate." Treating people like this will instill in them an indelible inclination to die for you in the future.

I ran a small speechwriter shop at GE—five or six writers and a couple admins. I used to pray for their success because I understood that it was inextricably linked to mine.

I ran the programs of all the big management meetings for the company as well and used to sweat and fret in the back of the cavernous room as some of the speakers, whom I had coached and rehearsed, mounted the stage and moved to the lectern. I knew that if someone failed, Welch would direct a glare at *me*.

The best and most successful people *want* everyone around them to succeed. If your significant compensation is stock based, you revel in your colleagues' successes and want everyone in the company to succeed. If that becomes your headset, your presentations will move from self-serving success stories about yourself, to *teaching* vehicles that share best practices, tips, and warnings with your colleagues.

Endnote

1. Geoff Colvin, "Nielsen's $78 Million CEO," http://money. cnn.com/2010/06/14/news/companies/David_Calhoun_ Nielsen.fortune/index.htm.

3 ——————————

Presiding Is Not Managing

Captain Smith's Deep Dive

Captain Edward John Smith, of the R.M.S. *Titanic,* was arguably the most experienced and skilled sailor aboard the brand-new ship he commanded. He had one more six-day cruise to New York to complete before retirement, after 40 years at sea. Yet he left the bridge of his ship, and its pleasant new paint smell, each meal time to dine in first class or his luxurious cabin, attended by his valet, as his liner raced recklessly (in retrospect) through the North Atlantic into a minefield of icebergs. The primitive but adequate "Marconi" of the time had already warned him about the bergs six or seven times.

On the night of the disaster, Smith delegated command of the ship to his first officer and then went to a dinner party *in his honor* thrown by the cream of 1912 society, most of whom would be fish food within hours.

He left the party early, went to the bridge to "check in" because of the approaching ice field, apparently reassured himself that he was "on top of things," and then went beddy-bye in his cabin, only to be awakened later by a grinding, crushing sound and the faltering heartbeat of the ship's engines.

He rushed to the bridge and learned that the first officer, Murdock, had been told by the crow's nest guy that the iceberg was "dead ahead" and had spun the helm and reversed the engines ("full astern") to miss the iceberg—or, I guess, hit it more gently.

This was a mistake, some have said. A ship that size could never have stopped in time or "bowed" before the iceberg. Its only hope would have been to swerve to avoid it—and reversing the engines and slowing the ship *decreased* its ability to do so (for reasons I think I understand but cannot explain). Full ahead and a spin of the helm to its stops could probably have allowed *Titanic* to miss the berg and live.

Would Captain Smith have done that if he had been at the helm or standing behind it? Would he have saved the ship?

Probably.

But he wasn't there.

He was having his ass kissed by his adoring passengers at his dinner party, after having "delegated" his responsibility to a subordinate and then putting on his jammies and hitting the sack in his luxury suite—as his ship, his responsibility, raced through an ice field.

What an egomaniacal, irresponsible, "hands-off" manager!

Captain Smith's "deep dive" was returning to the bridge after the collision woke everyone up and "isolating himself" from the nervous and scared officers, listening to the news that the ship was dying, and giving half-hearted orders, some of which were openly defied.

Some of these orders consisted of ambiguous commands to ready the lifeboats, but not at a pace that would alarm the doomed dopes that were wandering the decks after having placed their trust in "The Millionaires' Captain."

The band was ordered to play a bunch of snappy tunes to make everyone feel festive, warm, and comfortable, even though the more prescient of the passengers could feel the list in their feet and knew they had reservations for the Davy Jones cafe—downstairs.

A modern psychotherapist has opined that during this belated deep-dive, hands-on period, Smith was in a state of "temporary dysfunction" before he began his own deep dive—13,000 feet to the bottom of the Atlantic.[1]

Great dinner party, though! Smith must have been so honored, even as the icy ocean filled his nose and lungs.

Kip Condron of AXA-Equitable cites CEOs who spend too much time doing charitable stuff, raising funds for charities, and giving graduation speeches when they should be on the job—at the helm—in this ice field we are all steaming through.

Back to the Atlantic: Dive, Dive! Oops, This Isn't a Submarine

What should Captain Smith have done? Spent the whole six-day passage on the bridge? Monitored every detail? Steered the ship with his own hands as it entered the ice field?

Of course he should have!

During World War II, it was not uncommon for battleship captains to spend *three months at a time* on the bridge—eating, sleeping, poring over every detail, and never leaving—so that if the "balloon went up," they wouldn't be caught with their pants down in the "head" of a cabin below decks. They didn't want to have to explain at an inquiry why their ship hadn't zig-zagged when it was torpedoed or bombed, or why it had run into a friendly carrier because an idiot had been driving it while the captain was snoozing or taking a dump in his cabin.

Oofongo Rock and the Wreck That Never Happened

To do a speech and a magazine article for GE long ago, I spent a day touring a soon-to-be-launched Ohio-class Trident submarine, a vessel capable of virtually wiping out half of what was then the Soviet Union.

I spent a good part of the day guided by its captain, a man who was the absolute picture of confident, calm, resolute American leadership. An occasional flash of ferocity in his eyes implied disaster and dismissal for any officer or seaman under his command who didn't meet his standards of excellence or the codes he lived by and held all others to as well. He seldom smiled, yet in his focus on detail and principle, he reminded me a little of Jack Welch, without the raucous sense of humor (that's not an asset in an apocalyptic dealer of nuclear death.)

When he *did* smile, it was in recounting, with visible relief, a story of a near deep dive as we talked about leadership in his tiny quarters.

His attention to leadership detail was shaped by an instinctive decision he had made to save his last boat (a nuclear attack sub) and possibly the lives of him and his men. It relates to being situationally aware (in the terms used by the shrink I'd spoken to in describing cats). It's a brief story about listening to "what's going on" (or "smelling the shit," as we used to say in the Army), being in touch with the workings—the guts—of your business or organization, and listening to anyone with a worthwhile observation.

A brand-new seaman was in the conning tower, on his first tour on a nuclear sub. The captain and a few officers were with him as they sailed at high speed on the surface, on a dark, moonless night.

The seaman was doing some small job in the conning tower as the boat cruised off the coast of Japan.

Out of nowhere, this "kid" pointed to the paper navigation chart and the line on it that represented the sub's course. He pointed to a tiny dot, almost covered up by the pencil line, and asked, "What's that, sir?"

The captain, who normally didn't even make eye contact with someone of this man's rank, much less allow himself to be questioned by him, said (a little impatiently, as he told me), "What's what?" He watched as the seaman pointed to the dot.

Then the captain said, "Oh, my God!" (or words to that effect).

The "dot" the sailor had pointed to was a jagged solitary rock, Oofongo Rock, that sticks out of the sea. And it was *dead ahead* and only *minutes ahead.*

Orders were shouted, wheels (or whatever) were spun, and, minutes later, the crew watched with big eyes as Oofongo Rock loomed off the bow of the boat as it cruised safely by.

That seaman's curiosity about something totally "above his pay grade" and "outside his function," and the captain's willingness to listen and to swim deeply in every level of his responsibility rather than do an occasional "deep dive," probably saved a billion-dollar submarine, averted a massive radiation disaster, and preserved a few hundred lives.

The same captain told me that it was his policy to "cut" the bottom one or two performers after every cruise, to keep "upping" the quality of performance of his boat.

I suspect the "What's that, sir?" guy not only made the cut, but was possibly given the captain's cabin for the rest of the cruise, as the captain continued to exhale and thank his God for his instincts and his curiosity.

The Death of Mrs. Chippy

One of my favorite books is *The Endurance,* by Caroline Alexander, the story of probably the greatest adventure of all time. It tells of a World War I–era attempt to cross Antarctica on foot, an attempt that turned into a two-year nightmare when the adventurers' snug and well-provisioned ship became trapped in the pack ice short of where they were supposed to land. Over an extended period of time, the ship was crushed by the moving ice and sank, leaving them stranded more than a thousand miles from the nearest human habitation, a whaling station on South Georgia Island. They saw no other human being for two years, having been forgotten by a continent at war and after braving near-200mph winds, –100-degree temperatures, and malnutrition from a diet largely limited to seals and penguins. Amazingly, the adventurers had a photographer with them, and he managed to chronicle the story and bring most of his "plates" back to the world. *The Endurance* is a story that must be read, to round out an understanding of leadership and the human spirit.

The expedition loved animals—nearly 30 sled dogs and 1 cat, a pet, with no other function. "[They were] shot [serially] twenty-seven dogs in all. No more use was envisioned for them. The food they consumed had become too valuable; and their 'dog pemmican' [a kind of jerky] would become a staple of the crew's diet."[2]

When the mission became survival and escape somehow to the inhabited far north of this God-forsaken place, Sir Ernest Shackleton, perhaps the greatest explorer and one of the greatest *leaders* in history, told his men that the beloved animals were no longer of use; they *ate* food when they could *provide* it and must be disposed of.

Said one expedition member: "The duty fell upon me & was the worst job I ever had in my life. I have known many men I would rather shoot than the worst of the dogs."[3]

One of the men was tasked to kill his favorite dog, and his hands trembled so that he made a "botch" of it, as the Brits say, and had to fire again. The execution of Mrs. Chippy, the cat, caused a near-mutiny by her owner, whom Shackleton told, "Sorry, no pets."

You *must* get rid of the waste—and the losers and the nonproducers. And if you cannot, *you* will lose.

You can carry the waste—and go home, sleep well, play with your kids, and have a clear conscience—but that doesn't make you a winner. No one will hate you for a while. In fact, they may all love you. But you'll make losers of them as well as yourself, and the smart ones will come to realize it before too long.

Leaders sometimes have to destroy factories, close moribund businesses, and, let's be honest, hurt the towns and cities that host them.

Be sure you do this humanely—or as humanely as possible.

And if you believe in God, He will make you account for *how* you do it.

If you are not psychologically equipped to do this, you, like Jack Shaw of Hughes, need to do something else. In the military, that brass on your shoulder obligates you only to destroy the enemy. In business, you not only have to defeat the bad guys, but you sometimes have to obliterate some good guys as well.

And if you can't do it, you are sliding along like a leech. Your business—and, eventually, your company (and its employees)—will sink and die, with no "golden parachutes."

Incuriosity Kills the Dogs

Dennis Dammerman, the former chief financial officer and vice chairman of GE, is an old colleague with whom I shared (I think) a mutual respect. He told me once, as we worked on a graduation speech to his alma mater, that he wanted to tell the graduates that they must cultivate "an insatiable intellectual curiosity about everything around [them], and about everything for which [they] may someday be responsible." His advice: "If you are a nurse, understand how the hospital works, and then become familiar with the entire healthcare system [lotsa luck]. If you are a teacher, understand administration and the educational system and its problems." In other words, don't adopt a "hands-off" style.

Dammerman told me that he was amazed by the lack of curiosity he saw in many of the people he had worked with. He recalled looking forward with great pleasure to interviewing a senior manager of a semiconductor company GE had acquired in Silicon Valley.

He told me that one of the first things he had asked the man ("in good faith—it wasn't a trick question") was to give him an explanation of how a semiconductor works, in terms simple enough for another "finance guy" to understand.

Said Dammerman, "Turns out he hadn't a clue—not a *clue*—about the workings of the very product his company produced and [had] no curiosity whatsoever to find out. It was not a good interview."

I recounted in my last book, *Jacked Up*, that a Dammerman scalpel found nothing but air and feathers under a series of presentations made to him at NBC, and expounded on the resulting spectacular outburst of a critique that left one of the presenters crying next to the charts.

Incuriosity leaves you vulnerable to lies and dissembling. And unquestioned dissembling can destroy you or hurt your organization. Welch, who had the curiosity of a big cat, left himself open to being blind-sided only very infrequently.

I read the "Lynch Report" on the notorious fraud perpetrated by Joe Jett on a GE subsidiary, the now-defunct brokerage firm of

Kidder Peabody. I read it three times. At the end of the third read, I still couldn't understand how the hell it could have happened.

For those who don't remember the Joe Jett affair, a couple sentences are in order: In 1994, a young trader at Kidder made a series of bogus trades to inflate his own bonus. The fraud was perpetrated against the company instead of against customers, and it resulted in more than a third of a billion dollars in imaginary earnings. Those "earnings" were discovered only after the quarter's books were closed. The scheme was a distant but analogous relative of a Ponzi scheme: doomed to explode and be found out eventually.

Jett had been awarded "Man of the Year" honors at Kidder shortly before the incident. He disappeared when the scheme began to unravel. GE was forced to take a $350 million noncash charge against the quarter's earnings, a crushing blow that propelled Welch into his home bathroom to barf when told of it.

As Welch and I drove from the GE locomotive plant in Erie, Pennsylvania, one day, I said to him, "I still can't understand how this scheme could have gone on for so long."

"Incuriosity," he answered. "It was my fault. They gave him this award and this big bonus, and I never asked them exactly what it was for and why he could produce those numbers when no one else could."

I'd seen a video of Jett speaking at a Kidder Peabody meeting a while before this scandal broke. His rant took arrogance to the frontier of insanity. I think if Welch had seen it, he would have had further accounting inquiries made into Jett's "success."

Bob Nelson, a GE vice president who still does financial analysis work for Welch, told me, "You would lay out a deal for him [Welch], and he would dive into it, picking it (and you) apart, probing, questioning, erupting with yells that 'You don't know what you're talking about' or excited outbursts of 'Good, good! I love it!'—sometimes literally running around the room. And when you got out of there, you were sometimes pretty beaten up, but there was never a doubt that he knew the deal or the plan just about as well as *you* did by the time you left [or were carried out of] the room."

Contrast that with a conversation I had with a very senior financial executive who had left a major job at a major company because his plans and deals were seemingly of little interest to the CEO. "I used to lay out a multibillion-dollar deal, and after ten minutes he would say, 'Got it! Got it!' And I would walk out of there, saying to myself, "No, you *don't* fucking got it. You don't understand it."

Micromanaging—or, at least micro-understanding the workings of a business at every level—is, in my view, a characteristic of a winner.

Micromanage

I've claimed before, in other screeds, that Welch had the intellectual capacity and sense to micromanage at incredibly deep levels within the company *when necessary,* to actually add value. I still believe that meddling and *kibitzing* to a degree—and *always* when an organizational survival issue is involved—is a necessity, not an option.

If you are true to yourself and understand that you do not have the intellectual bandwidth (as the now-tired cliché goes), bring in that circle of trusted, well-paid friends and confidants. Send them out to sniff around, grasp, and digest for you the issues, the data, and any suspicions they may have. Then have them come back and feed them to you until you have an iron grip on the whole thing and are hyperbole-proof when you step into the briefing room with the people running the troubled, promising, or risky venture or business.

The first time or two you paralyze some feather merchant with an observation that flashes in the room like lightning at night, you will find that the bullshit stops. Its purveyors will begin to glance stealthily at each other: "Uh oh, can't fool this guy. Bag all those charts."

When you show, with a couple of animated and insightful comments (sarcasm is good), that you understand the issue and resent the disingenuous tone and content of this presentation—and that the next time you are the target of wool-pulling, the perps will be fired *on the spot*—straightforwardness and candor with the boss will no longer be an issue.

Mark Vachon disagrees with me on the "micromanagement" issue. His views should trump mine, since he was CEO of GE Medical Systems, Americas. My views are based on writing speeches for Welch, managing a few speechwriters, and running the major company meetings. But I was a pretty good close-up observer of management triumph and tragedy, hence this book.

In any case, Vachon says he does like to "go in the forest to look at the trees," but he disputes the fact that you should occasionally swim around like a catfish at the bottom of the organization. His view is, "Get into detail until you see a pattern; then tell the team, 'Here's where we're going.'" This coincides, tangentially, with Condron's view that you should get deep into the details until your gut tells you that you have someone in place whom you can implicitly trust for her judgment, integrity, and knowledge of the game; then get off her back and move on.

I cornered the British captain of a cruise ship at the captain's cocktail party, as we wandered pleasantly down the Caribbean. I told him the subject of this book and began a minor rant on how another Brit captain (Smith, by name) had attended a cocktail party in his honor as the ship sped through an ice field in the North Atlantic. He cut me off, with some irritation, and observed that no icebergs had been sighted recently in the Caribbean, that attending these functions was part of his ordered duties, and that he was on top of every function in the vessel he commanded. "How deep is your knowledge of the workings of the ship?" I asked pleasantly.

He replied with this brief story: Years before, he had boarded another cruise ship on his first assignment as a junior officer. As he wandered the decks in his immaculate white uniform, he noticed a frayed or broken cable on some piece of equipment. He called over one of the crew and asked him to fix it right away. The man replied, "You don't know how to splice a cable. Where do you get the right to tell me to do it?"

The young officer instructed the man to wait, went to his cabin and changed out of his white uniform into dungarees, and then returned. While the man watched, he proceeded to splice the cable (which, apparently, is no easy operation), getting greasy and filthy in the process. He then asked the deckhand to accompany him to the ship's first officer, described the man's disrespect and insubordination, and had him fired and thrown off the ship. (They were in port.)

The captain then politely dismissed me and moved to talk with less annoying passengers.

Former GE executive vice president Frank Doyle said, "Some leaders would drop everything else to "focus on one big thing—and then everything else would fall apart." He and vice chairman Paolo Fresco took over for Welch at the Corporate Executive Council meeting when Welch had health problems. He focused these people (the top 40 or so in GE, including the leaders of all the businesses) with these words, as he remembered them for me at lunch: "If there is ever a quarter where we *must* make the numbers, it is *this one*. Everyone understand that? If we 'miss,' everyone on the outside will say, 'This is a one-man band' [Welch]."

And they *did* make the numbers.

Good leaders put their heads down and do what *has* to be done, within the inflexible ropes of absolute integrity.

That reminds me of Infantry Officer's Basic Course. We saw a scenario painted of climbing a hill with our men, getting our asses shot off, calling in air support and artillery with no appreciable effect, and wondering aloud (or not) "Now what do I do?"

The answer, we were told, was, "Lieutenant, now is when you start earning your money."

Endnotes

1. Bradford Matsen, *Titanic's Last Secrets: The Further Adventures of Shadow Divers John Chatterton and Richie Kohler* (New York: Twelve, 2009).

2. Caroline Alexander, *The Endurance: Shackleton's Legendary Antarctic Expedition* (New York: Knopf, 1998), 115.

3. Caroline Alexander, *The Endurance: Shackleton's Legendary Antarctic Expedition* (New York: Knopf, 1998), 115.

4

The Imperative of Selective Micromanagement

Blondie's View

Former GE senior executive Bill Woodburn's view (and I envy him because he still has the blonde hair I had long ago, with no signs of losing it) is similar to mine. Naturally, that's why I agree with it. Bill feels that a key factor in losing is "superficiality," or managing "up" and at too high a level. He tells me, "A good leader has the ability to know how far to 'drive down.'"

Woodburn adds this important nuance to his obviously impassioned views: "When you are superficial in your vetting, it sends a message that you [in the organization] can be superficial in your analysis. When you know a review is going to be a 'cakewalk,' you know you don't have to be too rigorous in your analyses."

This slackness cascades down through the organization, spreading laziness, imprecision, and careless analysis. It manifests as bullshitting, lack of respect for the senior manager, and, eventually, organizational death.

When you are a good and winning manager, or an individual reporting to that manager, you get what Woodburn calls "butterflies" before the presentation. "On whose part?" I asked—the presenter or the presentee? His view was both. He compared a presentation to readying for a track meet and described the "but-terflies" as pleasant but electric ones that accompanied him as he stepped into the blocks and waited for the gun to go off. (I could empathize with the pitter-patter, having run track, but the tension I'd always felt related to whether I would come in last, or near it, as I usually did.)

"Superficiality leads you to decisions that I think are 'glossy'—made at too high a level, without real understanding of the data—and leads to decisions that do not account for key data, such as risk," he said. Without real diligence, the organization slides into a mindset of slack.

Woodburn quotes the aphorism, "The devil is in the details." You don't have to know all of them, but you do have to know the important ones.

At a Minimum, Develop a Bullshit Detector

Learn at enough depth that you cannot be deceived or get sold a load of feathers. One senior individual was a terrific presenter and spoke at one or two company meetings with sincerity and authority. He temporarily bamboozled even Welch and one or two of his senior lieutenants, but he couldn't dazzle some of the senior people who were familiar with his business. They only smirked, rolled their eyes, and came back again and again to the "bullshit" verdict over cocktails or dinner. That presenter got nailed sooner rather than later.

Fire people who try to deceive you. Fire them all. And do it loudly and publicly, with none of the usual biz-speak of "He left for personal reasons" or "to pursue other opportunities" or "to spend more time with family" or whatever.

How about: "We fired him because his values differed from ours. We wish him well."

I spent some time with Joe Plumeri, CEO of Willis Group Holdings (a major insurance-related company). Plumeri is a character. He dresses like John Gotti did, owns a couple minor-league baseball teams, talks with an unapologetic "Joisey" accent, and is fun to spend time with. He minces no words.

I reviewed a few of his speeches and saw a few videos of his many public speeches (he loves to do them) in preparation for meeting with him at his office across the street from the World Trade Center site.

I was amazed that, in one of his speeches, he made a point of mentioning the firing of a senior manager and big earner because of attitudinal and other issues. And he mentions him *by name*. This is almost never done in big-league business. I told him that I couldn't believe he had mentioned, publicly and recorded, the firing of a particular individual, especially an apparently talented one. He said matter-of-factly that the guy was undercutting many of the things he was trying to achieve (I forget the details), was bad with people, and, right to the point, was "an *asshole*." (That's also how he described the guy in his speech!)

I asked him why he would describe an admittedly good manager and good earner (as Tony Soprano would say) in that way. Plumeri answered, "Because he *is* an asshole." Good enough for me. Assholes should be fired. Don't allow yourself to become one—and don't tolerate them in your component.

At a general managers' meeting in the early 1990s, Welch specifically alluded to several executives who had been fired the previous year to underline the seriousness he attached to the values we were trying to develop in the company. This shocked some people, and a few people disapproved of the practice and thought it akin to kicking people who had already been knocked down, but it under-lined the seriousness of what he was trying to do.

Drilling Down

Frank Doyle, former GE executive vice president and head of relations (union, public, employee, government, and so on), told me that Welch pestered and "sniffed around" at various levels of the company, including the engine room and even the bilge. In some cases, this prompted all-night meetings and hen-house squawking and fluttering all over the GE world in preparation for one of his visits.

When Welch saw, smelled, or was told of something serious, drifting, problematic, or poorly led, he would "drill down on it and manage it, putting aside most other issues." (Doyle demonstrated by finger-drilling at his sandwich on the golf-club table.) One of these issues was the "dead-on-arrival X-ray tube" issue at GE, concerning a product failure that was embarrassing and tarnish-ing a flagship business. Welch leaped over the chain of command, including the head of the Medical Systems business CEO, fired and hired a bunch of people, immersed himself in the technology and processes, and then demanded (and, of course, received) *daily* reports on DOA rates until the problem, or series of problems, was resolved. Then he moved on.

Welch *micromanaged* the issue, which was way below his pay grade, to a successful conclusion.

But Frank Doyle continued, "All the other issues that were put aside temporarily while X-ray tubes or other issues got focused upon seemed to resolve themselves shortly thereafter." Maybe that was because of the passing shadow of the eagle overhead.

I've been wrestling with the "deep dive" issue for some time (and perhaps need to get a life), but my belief and my observation is that leaders who neglect detail and leave detail to others, and instead fly around giving graduation speeches and hosting endless United Way affairs, are "off the bridge," in Captain Smith's context. They're attending ceremonial events while neglecting the jobs for which they are paid outrageously.

Kip Condron, of AXA-Equitable, had perhaps a more reasonable view than mine. His view of how deep or shallow or wide a leader's attention span should be was that a leader needs to micromanage ("learn the business to its core") until he or she knows "who is good enough to be left alone."

Sounds reasonable, but how do you stay on top of things until you spot or smell a problem or opportunity that, in your view, isn't being addressed. This applies to all levels and all kinds of leadership.

Then do, if not a deep dive, at least a half-gainer, and stay on top of all issues of significance (or potential significance). Call those responsible for solving the problem, whether during the day or at home at night. If something smells funny or dangerous, learn it to its core, to the point that you can handle every question flung at you at an analysts' meeting or a congressional hearing.

I know I repeat myself here, but it is so important to winning and losing.

Nothing is more pathetic or more career- and company-threatening than seeing the boss (or a representative of an institution) relying on people whispering in his ear as he answers questions with "I'll have to get back to you on that" or "I'm going to let Mary handle that question—she's more familiar with that aspect of the manufacturing problems we're having with the dyno-wiget."

Questioners get impatient, opinions are formed, and you start to hear advice like, "Maybe we should have Charlie or Louise do the analyst meeting on the financial services issue. They're more on top of it, and you could probably handle the bigger picture and more general stuff." All that means, "You could probably do the figurehead stuff and let someone provide the substantive answers." That signifies an utter contempt for your leadership and the grasp you have of the issues you should be facing in your business, your battalion, your floor, or your component in the hospital.

You're being told something here: that you are a bumbler, an empty suit, an inadequate leader. You *can* turn around this looming Loser Express with constant interrogation and 14-hour days. And when you "drill down," as the cliché goes, you will be amazed at the stupid crap that goes on in your organization largely because of inertia, bad people, and bureaucracy.

Change it, lay your hands on it, swim in it. You will no longer be a figurehead, but a leader.

At the Pentagon a few years ago, a new brigadier general (handsome, young, with a fair combat record) was sent over to the Hill to testify on an Army weapons program. He saw the event as an honor and viewed himself as a "presider," with a gaggle of lieutenant colonels responsible for knowing the data. He brought his wife to the hearing as a date, handed off almost all questions to "back-ups" (the aforementioned colonels), and said "We will provide that" to the ones he answered.

Eye-rolling and impatient gestures from the congressmen and committee staff followed, along with some sarcasm about "lack of data." The general returned to the "Puzzle Palace" (the Pentagon, where we worked), to be chewed out by a three-star general for not being prepared. "You are *never* going up there again." The "committee reviews" had been phoned in to the Pentagon: "Don't send him over here again." Bringing his attractive wife as a date was mentioned with disgust.

His career dribbled off and terminated. The guy was a lightweight.

You may have different views of the degree of involvement in and knowledge of a business or component that a leader must have.

I do, but I tend to favor "in depth" over the fake, superficial grasp of the function the figurehead has.

Andrew McMahon, of AXA, may have cut the Gordian knot with his view, "You must have the depth of understanding of the business that you can smell bullshit like a shark smells blood in the water."

"He Looked Like an Emperor Until He Actually Became One" —Tacitus

One of the more interesting losers, in my observation, was a senior business leader who "considered himself above the fray," in the view of Bob Nelson, a GE vice president. "A lot of people fail because they spend too much time on one thing. This guy spent time on *nothing* and was phenomenal at disguising his uninvolvement."

As Nelson described it, "His view of the 'big job' was [taking] luxurious travel, being waited upon, [earning an] awesome compensation, and enjoying the trappings of senior leadership without the work of understanding what he was leading."

"Uninvolved" emperors or empresses (at any level) usually design elaborate and sometimes clever mechanisms to protect themselves from the vulnerabilities and snickers caused by their feckless or disconnected behavior.

Doyle recalled a planned edict of a dollar-an-hour-wage reduction at an embattled GE industrial business. The above-the-fray business leader had signed off on the proposal. The union was absolutely thrilled!

Doyle hated it because the reductions applied only to the people who actually "made things" (electric motors), not to the "professionals," and certainly not to the "executives" in the business.

The business leader who actually knew very little about the business—it was boring, in his view, and not that important—utilized his unquestioned intelligence to construct escape mechanisms that would kick in when the torches and pitchforks came out. He would be well in back of the ramparts as Welch's and/or Doyle's heads were carried around ceremonially on pikes.

This is inevitably a losing behavior.

At least for a couple more years, this uninvolved manager was *promoted* after the "dollar-an-hour" thing was resolved. But he later fireballed the new bigger job when no one could deny his arrogance and detachment—even Welch, who liked him.

In the meantime, however, he had acquired a Ferrari, a Lamborghini, a big-time BMW, and *two* hand-made $100,000 shotguns.

Most of the people who worked for him expressed a wish that he would "eat" one of them.

5

Dithering and Distractions

"Intuitiveness" on Naked Emperors

Steve Bennett, former CEO of Intuit and an old friend of mine, says, "People who manage for the short term to get promoted lose credibility because everyone knows what they are doing."

The Emperor has clothes, but they are transparent.

The "little engine" of their ambition is visible to all.

Bennett says, "They focus on their promotion rather than stewardship, and their 'brand' suffers."

Cost-cutting is a necessary component, even a fixation, for leaders who are interested in succeeding. But there must be other "fixations." Any fool with an HR staff of "button people" and a perceived mandate can lead a "Sherman's march" through a business, burning and pillaging and piling up the bodies. Admittedly, shareowners usually love it. Often this approach plays well with people who admire the "tough-guy approach," who Bob Nelson, a former GE vice president, calls "suckers for the breed."

But this *inevitably* fails and leads to disaster and ridicule *if that is the leader's only dimension.* Another one-trick pony winds up on top of the pile of bodies he shot.

Jack Welch emphasized cost-cutting and its more graphic synonym *takeouts* (of personnel) during his 20 years as CEO, earning him the "Neutron Jack" label (which he hated—or claimed to hate). We worked endless hours preparing his CEO letter at the front of the annual report, but the letter *he* quoted most, in my memory, was the one from the chairman of Toyota, who wrote, as I recall, "We will take out cost as we have never taken out cost before." Welch sent the Toyota letter to every general manager–level executive and officer in the company, with a "request" that they meditate on what we were up against.

But Welch never paraded around the Neutron Jack thing. He preferred to focus on positive initiatives: acquisitions, Six Sigma, quality, globalization, and so on. All acts get old, and although Welch stuck with the stuff that got him there, he was always open to new things—if they made sense. The electronic revolution and "e-business" came hard for him because he was getting older and suspected (rightly, in many cases) that much of it (the dot-com stuff) was an evanescent trend, which it was. But when he saw the light, he leapt on the boat with the ferocity that characterized every other one of his enthusiasms.

Once again, the "one-tricks" inevitably seem to crash and wreck. "Chainsaw Al" Dunlap just hacked and slashed, and seemed to revel in doing so. He wound up hearing people cheering and laughing as he was led off to jail for other stuff. Bob Nardelli, a good man, simply brought his GE cost-cutting toolkit with him to Home Depot ("Why do we need 'greeters'"?) and found that those tools, by themselves, were not enough to get the job done.

Philanthropy as Palliative

The cornered, insecure, diffident manager (whether scared or in denial and over his or her head) sometimes finds comfort in the folds of the comfortable robes of social interaction, charity, or philanthropy. It's certainly easier than the more painful, onerous, arduous, and risky business of getting his or her arms around responsibilities, firing people, making choices, and getting the mess out.

The socially responsible stuff is easy. But it's not why you were given the job. Without rancor or sarcasm, Kip Condron points to Paul O'Brien of New England Telephone, who spent "too much time on charities" at the expense of leading the business. Nothing ignoble about that—possible rewards in heaven, certainly a lot of applause and good publicity for the company, along with nice press clips. But to be frank, Wall Street could care less about your support of the crippled children's fund, how diverse your board is, or how "green" you are becoming. You can wave the flag at the big events and give great speeches, but don't spend the meat of your time jetting around to backslap if your business isn't roaring ahead—or even if it is. Let your executives take turns talking to "causes" and sharing a little bit of their time with these various groups.

Steve Bennet says, "I have seen many people in Silicon Valley, and some 'failed' GE people, that seemed to have been focused on the 'social aspects' and 'relationships' rather than on business results." Socially responsible initiatives and advertising are wonderful PR, but if your share owners are suffering, play it down or cut it out entirely. Stick to promoting your products, not how great *you* are."

AXA-Equitable, which has a gorilla that I occasionally find tedious in its commercials, is nevertheless engaged in a hard sell: The "gorilla in the room" is reminding you of your worst nightmares: growing old and crazy and eating out of dumpsters behind the Stop & Shop because you didn't get AXA financial products while you still had time.

The trappings, accolades, and "Best Company to Work For" stuff is nice. Campaigns such as Ecomagination, with beautifully done and hugely expensive commercials, may make your employees feel warm until they look at their 401(k)s, with their languishing stock price. Then the big chill returns.

To repeat: "Best Company to Work For" awards are nice, but if the business isn't doing well and the stock price is lower than the proverbial snake's belt buckle, everything else is tinsel. Ask any analyst.

Politely decline events with the Chamber of Commerce, the United Way, and all the other groups. You can write some checks, corporate and personal, if you'd like. That's really all they're interested in anyway. Before you accept a speaking engagement, evaluate it with a stringent criterion screen of "How will this benefit the company?"

Welch turned down perhaps one speech or appearance invitation a day when he was CEO. He focused relentlessly on employees, press, and financial analysts. He did the big speeches, to customer groups and people who could become customers; he either passed on the rest or asked one of his officers to fill in for him.

Look askance at appearance requests, especially if they involve travel and significant preparation. Screw the graduation speeches, unless it's for your alma mater. Focus on what you are paid for: winning and growing shareowner wealth. Sound grubby? Maybe. It's just one view—or maybe not, since an array of CEOs have been eased out because of long-term stock languishment.

Tiptoe People

I covered the topic of self-confidence in my previous book. Welch, from whom I learned it (although I had a visceral understanding of it from time in the Army, particularly combat time) speaks of it in his first book. But it is such a *sine qua non* for failure avoidance that it cannot be glossed over.

The hero in T. S. Eliot's immensely depressing poem *The Love Song of J. Alfred Prufrock* is riddled with insecurities over his bald spot, whether he should "eat a peach," and, most characteristically, something I have actually felt in the distant past: "missing the point" in a conversation with someone of "importance," someone you'd like to interest or be taken seriously by. "That is not it at all. That is not what I meant at all," says Eliot.

And the crestfallen, blushing, crushed, self-confidence-deficient loser smiles in a sickly fashion and falls silent.

He should be saying, "Well, screw you. That's *exactly* what I meant." And then he should back it up with some views and data as soon as the big shot regains his or her color and composure.

> *Should I part my hair behind? Do I dare to eat a peach?*
> *I shall wear white flannel trousers and walk upon the beach.*
> *I have heard the mermaids singing, each to each.*
> *I do not think they will sing to me.*

People like Mr. Prufrock tiptoe through life over eggshells and dread decisions or interactions because they are not sure whether they really know their business or responsibilities.

They have gone over the Peter Principle edge and are in over their heads, without the flotation of wise counsel, good advice, and good friends.

What's the solution to the self-confidence issue?

Know everything that can be known about a venture, a move of any importance, or a personnel hire of any significance. Take your best advice from people you trust. Fire anyone you have determined, through data, that you cannot trust.

The French have a saying: *"L'audace; l'audace. Toujours l'audace!"* It became seemingly inoperative after a few early rounds in World War II, but it's generally good advice: Always attack—or, rather, make "attack" your predisposition.

A man I have no connection with but who has long had my sympathy was a Navy captain (of the cruiser *Chicago*) in the World War II battle of Guadalcanal, in which the United States Navy suffered the worst defeat in its history.

The captain, Howard Bode, took his ship into battle, where it suffered moderate damage: a torpedo near the bow. Apparently, he thought the safety of the ship (which was not in mortal danger, by any means) dictated "withdrawing" from the raging fray. So he withdrew.

After the stinging naval defeat at the hands of the Japanese, an inquiry criticized Bode for his actions (which you can read as cowardice but most certainly were not). Humiliated, Bode shot himself and died.

Solution? Almost always *attack*.

They needed that cruiser in the battle.

He "withdrew."

Don't be *too* stupid. But as we used to say, if you are going to be a bear, you might as well be a grizzly!

Consult with your confidants, listen to their counsel, quickly balance it with your insights and instincts, and *go*. You may get bloodied, you may fail, or you may get fired. But you will know that you are a player, and, win or lose, the self-confidence will come with it.

Everyone else will sense it, too.

Don't get involved in a post-mortem with a higher-up on a failed venture or decision and not come across as knowing, down to the nuts and bolts, what prompted your decisions. If you are a skimmer scooting across the surface and that becomes evident (as it will) you will (and should) be fired.

And any organization that sheds a leader for making a well-thought-out move that does not work out, is a place you don't want to be anyway.

Here, as in most human behaviors, there seems to be a Peter Principle frontier. Too little self-confidence *inevitably* leads to failure. Too much of it sometimes—but not always—leads to the hubris that can cause the arrogance that Boeing's McNerney says is at the root of most "flameouts."

Welch readily admits that he got "Too full of [himself]" after years of meteoric success and the RCA acquisition. As a result, he bought Kidder Peabody, a Wall Street snake pit that gave all of us a (minor and temporary) black eye. He seemed to have a relapse with the aborted Honeywell merger attempt just before his retirement; the merger attempt was done pretty much on impulse and whim.

A bloody nose will not earn you the same self-esteem as a success. But if it's boldly done, the result is almost as good. And you'll probably never tiptoe again.

Tom Meyers, founder and former CEO of CQMS, in Australia (and worldwide), specifies "presence" as a *sine qua non* of a leader who can survive and prosper. I've met a lot of people in my career, some with presence and some without. Some of the ones with presence blew up and crashed. But I can't think of too many without presence who ever really went anywhere. Scientists, lawyers, and finance people can lack presence and make great careers in their games, but they never seem to break out into reaching range of the big brass rings that come with successful leadership of men and women.

You may be saying, "Okay, Lane, I bought this book, and I am a quiet, bespectacled guy or a meek young woman, and I realize I do not have 'presence.' When I walk into a room, I do not inspire the instant hush or generate smiles or friendly nods that are a tribute to presence. So what should I do?"

How the hell should I know? Kidding.

Actually, I have a few experience-based views.

- Get self-confidence. Once you have it, it radiates from you like ET's heart. Take an impossible assignment, work 16 hours a day, neglect your family as much as necessary, get rid of "bad" people, and win or lose. Either way, you are going to be a different man or woman. Welch used to say that self-confidence was the key to everything, and he kind of ceased talking about it after a couple big wins gave him the presence to walk into a big room full of big-shots and hold sway. I doubted myself as a confident officer in the Army until I got thrown into the Tet offensive in Vietnam, did nothing notable, got my guys back safe, and helped kick some North Vietnamese ass. Instant self-confidence! "I can do this!"

- Learn how to communicate. I know I've beaten this to death (and I will beat it further later), but a leader who stands up and drones about some "targets" his finance guy gave him, barfing numbers from an absurdly complex PowerPoint nightmare, inspires no one.

- The thoughts have to come from the leader, as do the passion and fire. I *helped* Jack Welch with his speeches, letters, and other communications for the better part of two decades, but it was all him. I wordsmithed, organized, and contributed some phrases and a thought or two, but it was all him. And everyone *knew* it was all him. If I'd implied to anyone otherwise, I would have been out of there the next day.

I read other CEO speeches and annual report letters and other communications (as much as I can take). I find it both interesting and disappointing that an individual is simply getting reading or signing off on some communication written by a grunt like me. Why don't they write their own stuff? If they don't think it's a "good use of their time" to frame their own thoughts, even with some rhetorical help, then fire them out of there. Employees, and especially senior reports, know exactly whose thoughts are being presented.

When GE was looking to hire someone for the job I eventually got (formerly "Manager, CEO Communications"), Welch said indignantly, "*I'm* the manager of CEO communications." And he remained so. It contributed, along with his performance and wolverine personality, to a persona and presence that continues long past his retirement.

He is intense and never boring.

Presence.

6

Arrogance

Big Shots

The GE jet came in on a business flight with its cargo of two executives: one a plain old vice president and the other a senior vice president. (*Note:* GE, a company that pays 300,000 to 400,000 employees, has fewer than 200 vice presidents and probably an average of 20 senior vice presidents.)

The GE hangar was at White Plains Westchester County Airport in New York. The two men disembarked into the waiting GE town car.

The senior vice president lived in Fairfield, Connecticut, about 45 minutes or so from the airport. The plain old vice president lived in Greenwich, Connecticut, down the road from Fairfield, but only 10 to 15 minutes from the airport.

The senior vice president instructed the driver to drop him off first. So they made the long trip to Fairfield, dropped off the big shot, and then turned around and drove another 40 minutes back to Greenwich to drop off the junior guy.

Would you do this? Can you envision yourself doing anything remotely like this someday?

If you can see yourself, for a moment, *ever* doing this—treating people like crap because it is within your power—rethink. Big-shot behavior without superstar performance is a source of almost inevitable losing.

My (true) story is, admittedly, a ridiculous tempest in a teapot, with a millionaire being forced to ride in a limo an extra hour (worse tragedies have happened in world history). But it is absurdly illustrative.

Here's an even better example.

Picture this scene: A big-shot senior vice president was holding court over several lesser managers (senior mid-level to senior, but not officer level). The subject of Stan came up. The senior vice president was fueled, as was everyone at this point, by multiple martinis and listened to the critical views of the sycophants at the table piling on Stan. He sucked down another drink; it was now elevenish at night. The Beefeaters and pomposity-loaded big shot turned to Joe, who had been defending his subordinate, Stan, from the criticism of the drunken jackals.

"Joe," he said, "I want you to call Stan *right now* and fire him.

"But I can't do that. Can't we wait and talk this over? This guy really isn't bad at all, and he's in his early 50s."

"You go find a phone and fire him right now. Do it."

Joe was distraught. But instead of firing an "f-bomb" at this big shot, he found a pay phone and called poor Stan, who was either asleep or about to go to sleep. There would be no sleep after this call. The big shot hath murdered sleep.

Joe, the coward (who probably had kids in college and a mortgage himself), said, "Stan, I have to fire you." He then rambled on semicoherently and apologetically.

Stan, recognizing the signs of an alcohol-fueled conversation, said, "Why don't we talk about this tomorrow?"

In a whining voice amid sniffling, Joe told Stan he was fired and again apologized profusely, shifting the onus to the big shot, where it belonged, but not mentioning that he hadn't had the courage to tell the big shot to stuff himself.

The next day, in the light (or twilight) of hangovers and well-earned guilt feelings, the firing was "taken back" and Stan was allowed to continue his limp toward the retirement finish line.

The big shot, by the way, a creation of the previous chairman, was fired by Jack Welch shortly thereafter, for a variety of reasons—one of them for being the type of guy who would do what I just described.

"Come with Me": Arrogance Morphs into Bizarre Behavior

This story is about a brilliant man wandering his domain in a fog of self-absorption. He consented to have several lower-level professionals pitch him on some deal. He listened, languid and noncommittal, for a while. Then he announced that he had to "go." He flopped out of his chair and said, as an addle-pated afterthought, "Come with me."

These three or four (fortunately, all male) trooped into the men's room. The big shot entered a stall and, accompanied by "1812 Overture" sound effects, loudly continued the discussion of whatever.

I have never even *heard* of too many people like this who come to a good end. Many (most) wind up with a ton of money but have to endure their kids being mocked for what a jerk their father (or, in some cases, mother) is. The kids generally don't wind up so great, either.

Arrogant, big-shot behavior takes many forms. Some are less nasty and *outré* than others, but almost all lead to Train Wreck Junction.

A very senior executive went to Taiwan to see important Chinese customers (whom he considered a pain in the ass). He found out that the Taiwanese had scheduled an eight- to ten-course meal in his honor, with important government officials attending. The executive was being treated for what turned out to be a *faux* heart condition and believed this was too much food. At 5:00 the night of the dinner, he ordered his people to arrange for the number of courses to be cut to *two*. He angered everyone, particularly the customers.

He also had his company fly cases of bottled water to China, Japan, Korea, and Taiwan so he wouldn't have to drink "contaminated" stuff. He serially insulted customers, whose water (at least, their bottled water) was probably purer than American water.

Then he did the diva thing in China. He was supposed to meet with several senior government officials on very big deals. Instead, he couldn't be coaxed from his room. Panicky calls took place until a replacement executive was found. No explanation was given.

This executive returned to his lavish American headquarters and briefed his senior staff of 20 or 30 people. He regaled them with a lengthy, hugely self-serving, and totally false recitation of his activities and accomplishments on the Asia trip, nodding periodically to the vice president who had accompanied him, for reinforcement and embellishment of a story that was totally bogus.

The vice president who described this trip and this meeting for me said he had sat there dumbfounded and agape. "Everything he said was total bullshit."

This kind of behavior was rare at GE and was only barely tolerated if it was accompanied by smash-mouth business performance. The minute the performance went south, the guy was gone.

Smoke Break: The Pleasures, Triumphs, and Tragedies of Occasional Recreational Arrogance

About a decade or so ago, smoking provided an outlet for occasional harmless assertion of rank and status. Today the smokers themselves have become a source of satisfaction for the superior people who pass them in the doorways of office buildings, freezing, and still act out their detestation with hand waving and other signs of disgust if they catch a whiff of their indulgence. The glassed-in, hermetically sealed smokers' rooms in the airports that still allow such things delight the supercilious, morally superior travelers who rush by and cluck with amused pity at the 10 or 20 poor souls standing in the tobacco haze, having a "quick one" or two before boarding. Kind of like the "normal people" in the Britain of long ago who used to pay to watch the lunatics at the Bedlam asylum gibber and careen off the walls.

Smoking is so disapproved of today that it furnishes almost no opportunities for the demonstration of recreational arrogance. It has been banned indoors at most public buildings and is now prohibited *anywhere on the campuses* of many, if not most, corporate locations. The lowly gardeners, delivery men, and kitchen workers are left with one fewer pleasurable break in their sometimes dismal lives. A few decades ago, when the vice was in limbo, smoking still provided some pleasurable opportunities for status assertion. I boarded a small corporate helicopter flight with the company medical director (not an officer), who abhorred smoking and tried to dissuade the executives he treated from pursuing it further. A vice president boarded with us, and I had trouble keeping from laughing when, as we lifted off, he fired up a cigarette. The kindly old doctor sat, mortified, across from the vice president in the tiny helicopter cabin for the 20-minute flight to the airport where one of the company jets was waiting to take us to the annual shareowners' meeting.

Our vice president was the senior individual on the helicopter, bound for the plane where he would be one of the *junior* individuals and where smoking would be prohibited for the two-hour flight. Hence, the smoking lamp was lit on the way.

On the way back from the meeting, I was on the plane with only one other individual, a vice chairman, and one of the few remaining smokers at corporate. We knew each other fairly well and sat across from each other in the large plane. At liftoff, the pack of Marlboros came out, after a quick look at me asserting status and privileges. I was an off-and-on moderate smoker and was unbothered by it, so I quickly made a surprise move (with my pawn), and asked "Can I have one of those?" Disarmed and delighted, he held out the pack. He and I laughed, drank good wine, and smoked happily on the way back home, a bonded brotherhood of carcinoma.

He recounted, for our mutual pleasure, a story combining regal arrogance and revenge that he described as providing him with great satisfaction. It seems his daughter was nearing the final hurdles to admission at an Ivy League university and had an appointment to be interviewed one evening by an alumnus at his home as part of the rigorous and selective process leading to acceptance. The senior vice president and his wife dropped the nervous girl at the curb in front of the alumnus's house and orbited for a time nearby, awaiting her departure after the interview finished. After a while, they saw her moving hurriedly down the walk with an air of distress about her that her mom and dad saw immediately. They were shocked as she got into the car to see that she was in tears and nearly hysterical. "I'm not getting in the school," she said. "He interviewed me, and at the end, he said, 'I know what our school can do for you. I don't know what you can do for the school.'" That was the end of interview, the dash of hopes, and the beginning of hysterics.

Time passed, and our vice chairman (then a senior vice president and CEO of a major GE business) was seated at his desk, preparing for a routine "final interview" of an outside-GE candidate for a senior position in his business. Previous interviews by his lieutenants up the chain had all gone well, and the recommendations were positive.

And then a light went on as he reviewed the man's pedigree.

This was the alumnus who had arrogantly crushed his daughter that night!

Revenge being a dish enjoyed better cold, as the saying goes, he conducted the interview of the smiling candidate, nodding and responding cordially to his answers.

Then at the conclusion, he said, "You know, I know what GE can do for *you*, but I'm not sure what *you* can do for GE." As the awful realization of who he was crossed the man's face, he said, "Now get the fuck out of my office."

What we have here is a story brimming with beauty and symmetry: a pompous toad employing his arrogance as a self-satisfying end in itself to unnecessarily inflict anguish on a young woman; and the righteous cold wrath of a father, with the power to do so, employing a form of arrogance to blister and crush a malefactor who deserved it.

Sometimes arrogance can be a beautiful thing, if not indulged carelessly or too frequently.

Fit or Finish

Bob Nardelli is not an old friend, and I've worked closely with him only maybe twice a year on his presentations at major GE meetings. I liked him, in a way—which has no meaning nor bearing on anything.

I did not think he belonged in the same intellectual arena as the two other "contendas" for the job as CEO of GE, arguably the biggest prize in the corporate world. He's brilliant—smarter than I am—but we are navigating a GE universe of IQ that dwarfs other galaxies.

The race for the prize was not a sham—something between a real race and a compulsory show. Welch never tipped his hand, nor head faked, nor allowed a face that was not made for poker to give away his thoughts. I remember when I first began writing speeches for Welch, I sent him a draft speech for some long-forgotten occasion and was making my way into the auditorium at corporate headquarters when I spotted him rounding the corner about 40 yards away and headed for the same place. He spotted me as soon as I spotted him, and a baleful scowl came over his face. He'd obviously hated the draft I'd sent him. I figured, as I made my way to my seat in the auditorium, "Well, this gig isn't gonna last too long." He has the *opposite* of a poker face.

But many of us then, and many senior people today, guessed he had all but made his mind up on who the next chairman was going to be maybe a year and a half before, and that Jeff Immelt was the guy. In fact, Nick Heyman, one of the senior analysts who follows GE, announced that the race was "Jeff's to lose." We asked him to please stop saying that, because it was fueling the race mentality we were trying to avoid. But some of us believed it ourselves. In one of the more fascinating parts of his first book, Welch details the elaborate and theatrical moves he engineered to keep the cat in the bag.

He even wrote, years before, to his senior managers, that he hated the "horseshit" that accompanied the "race." And he refused, with some coldness, to engage in any conversations where he might let an "impression" of his slip.

Phil Rizzuto told me one day, over a delightful lunch at the club at Yankee Stadium, with a whole bunch of intoxicated *gindaloons* yammering "Scooter!" from the balcony above us, "There was one way to lose Joe DiMaggio as a friend and have him never speak to you again. Mention Marilyn Monroe." Welch wasn't that extreme, but none of us at my level, nor at levels above me (and there were plenty of those), ever got a thing out of him on the race. A couple times, I threw out a few views (always favorable) about one of the "contendas." Welch either didn't comment or did so briefly and blandly and then jostled me peremptorily to the business at hand (probably a speech or annual report CEO letter).

We finally gave up.

The rationale for a *three*-way race was a combination of typical Welch self-reference. That's how *he* had been chosen as CEO, and look how great that had turned out. A two-man race could be a bloodbath, a nonproductive waste of company time, and a media feeding frenzy that would resemble the two-horse showdowns that Sea Biscuit starred in 1930 at Belmont and Santa Anita.

I realize there's not a global demand for rehashing a GE CEO succession race of a decade ago, but its results illustrate, to a degree, how "fit" is so important to career at any level.

First of all, any leader of a P&L business within a company who gets the nod to be CEO faces an enormous "fit" issue. He must deal with so much dreck that he has zero experience with. It almost supports an argument for a prospective CEO candidate to be chief operating officer for a couple years, effectively running the company on a leash of any length deemed prudent by the CEO. If that person wasn't suitable, a shift to a major business leadership position within the company, with suitable hoopla and compensation, could be engineered and a new COO could be installed. At one point in the 1990s, Welch considered making Larry Bossidy his soul mate and most trusted *compadre*, the president of GE, with Welch staying as chairman.

Two problems: Bossidy was about Welch's age and could not become chairman if Jack retired at 65 (which he did). Bossidy instead left to become CEO of Allied Signal (later Honeywell).

The point is that Welch had enough self-awareness of his own personality and knowledge of Bossidy's equally powerful persona that, inevitably—and probably before long—there would be blood on the floor of the board room when these two titanic egos and wills clashed.

It seems to me that one must ask oneself, when promoted into a big job, whether one fits that job.

Media Madness and Untimely Death

The participants in these races are generally heavily interviewed by the press, if they consent, and cannot say stupid and ultimately career-killing things. Tom Vanderslice was a senior executive, a superstar, and someone very much in the running in the semifinals of the GE succession race that Welch ultimately won.

But he decided to give an interview to a major business magazine, in which he made some comments indicating that if he didn't get the big job, he would leave GE. This was widely perceived as "arrogant," from board level to the executive rank and file, and Vanderslice's race was over. Shortly thereafter, he departed GE for GTE.

Loose lips, perceived arrogance, and "thinking aloud" can kill your career at any level. I like the media (some of my best friends are what used to be called "ink-stained wretches"), but they can kill ya. Keep your mouth shut, remain an enigma, and comment only on business issues, never your personal ambitions. The media can kill you if you misspeak and there's very little upside for you, even if you don't say something untoward or dumb.

We had a midlevel media manager at GE's jet engine business years ago. A jet fighter plane crashed, and engine failure was the preliminary indication. Media called our manager at GE and asked what might be the cause of the presumed engine failure. Instead of saying, "How the hell should we know? We don't fly the planes— the Air Force does. Go talk to the Air Force," he began to ruminate on things that "might be" the cause, engine components that had failed in the past, possible broken fan blades, and more. All of that was gratefully reported.

The jet fighter wasn't the only thing that crashed that day.

The GE vice chairman under whom the aircraft engine business was located had a cow when he saw the press and wanted the manager fired immediately. He was dissuaded temporarily, but the manager's career "flamed out," and he left a while later.

In the meantime, he had to know of the parodies of his interviews that had begun to circulate around corporate headquarters. One of them went, "'Joe, when asked why the engine may have failed, leaned back in his chair, inserted his foot in his mouth, lit up a wingtip, and began to speculate: 'Well, it could be any one of a number of things we've had problems with in the past with this engine. I don't know. The pumps could have failed; the compressor may have blown up....'"

From then until his departure, he was widely known as "The Shoe Man." Very few people have ever gotten hurt by keeping their mouths shut.

In the few instances I was interviewed at GE (remember, I was a speechwriter, a ghost), I found myself drifting toward dangerous waters in an effort to be a "good interview." But then the alarm bells went off, and I moved away from the shoals with some self-effacing statement that I knew nothing about what was being asked, that it was "above my pay grade," and that I was a mere "word assistant" to the chairman.

That stuff doesn't sell magazines, but it keeps careers, at whatever level, aloft—or, rather, it keeps them from crashing catastrophically, at least for the moment. If you must be interviewed (and it will typically be about something "bad" that happened), you cannot clam up or say something stupid, like "No comment"; even generally friendly media will career off the reservation and feel given a license to write any crazy sensational nonsense (usually negative nonsense) that will create comment and sell articles. You've got to say something. But you must keep setting the agenda, not the reporter or a financial analyst on the phone in the wake of some kind of glitch.

Occasionally, I listened to Joyce Hergenhan, our vice president of public relations, and Bruce Bunch, head of press relations, give interviews on the phone. They continuously steered the interview and set its agenda, sometimes a bit sternly. For example: "The Company has had 27 (or 40 or 12) quarters of double-digit earnings, and you want to talk about why we did only 9% in the trough of a recession? Why don't you go talk to X or Y or Z companies that were flat or lost money? I don't understand your point. We're over here celebrating this rate of growth in a recession, and you want to write a story about the most successful company in America growing only 9%? Who gave you this story to write, because it makes no sense?"

L'audace; l'audace, tourjours l'audace!

7

Reality

Get Real or Get Out

The delusional behavior that sticks in my mind is the group suspension of disbelief of the GE nuclear systems business some two-and-a-half decades ago. This group had meetings and produced beautiful strategic planning books claiming that the projected sales and earnings of this once-great GE division that produced reactors made electricity that was "too cheap to meter": "Three reactors this year; more next." That was Kool-Aid talk, and it never happened, of course. Jack Welch gave the fish eye, and worse, to the execs who "pitched" the next year's business fantasy to him. He made them stop and turned their faces toward the reality that there would be no new nuclear reactor orders in the United States—maybe forever, and at least in their lifetimes.

One way to avoid losing is to see the world as it really is, not how you would like it to be. Once again, this recalls the McNerney formula of gathering friends around you who will tell you the way the world really is rather than pitch it in the delusions of your dreams and reveries.

In a speech I helped him with, and in his book with Ram Charan, titled *Execution*, Larry Bossidy tells the story of a friend who ran a half-billion-dollar division that made products for industrial markets. Customers had told Bossidy's friend that their sales were down because of competition from foreign suppliers. The customers were under crushing pressure to reduce their costs of manufacturing and doing business.

That friend said that his customers had repeatedly told him that they needed to reduce costs drastically. One customer told him that he'd just dropped a long-standing component supplier for one based in China, and a few of this guy's customers had themselves *moved* to China.

His team sat down to put together their strategic plan and prepared what they saw as a tough response to their view of reality. They would close one of their four U.S. plants, consolidate their three European plants into two, grind down on expenses and costs, and increase R&D spending to keep their products ahead of the pack.

But it took the new CFO to "write something nasty on the wall," to paraphrase Stevie Wonder. He said, "You are heading down the wrong track. This is not cyclical change. It is *structural* change. Total change. You have to have global cost parity. You can't be out of line with the lowest-cost source, no matter how good your product is."

Then he said, "You need to move your whole operation to China."

Bossidy and Charan described the man as sitting there in silence as reality pressed its crushing weight upon him. He remembered the hints his friends and customers had dropped about moving toward China-based suppliers.

Reality was sinking in—and it stunk.

The story included a look out the plush conference room window as the shift changed and seeing a great American workforce walk out laughing and kidding each other on the way home to see their kids—kids the CEO's kids played with, kids he'd coached in

Little League, kids he probably went to church with and who heard the same sermons on social responsibility and the Golden Rule.

They began the move to China.

All those employees streaming out of the plants would be streaming on to the unemployment lines. He felt like crap. And Pat Buchanan and a bunch of other populists, some of whom I like and respect, would say he *should* feel like crap since he is part of the destruction of the American economy and way of life.

I don't know. As a leader, you can sit and collect your stock option cash, ride around in helicopters, and preside over the sinking of your *Titanic*, like that ridiculous Captain Smith. And you can retire, and hit the beach in some theme-park community in Florida as the company founders and the guys that mill, or grind, or mix stuff in your plants lose everything.

But if you move to China, won't they lose it also?

Yeah, maybe.

No, probably. They will not be accompanying the business.

Face reality or face the firing squad.

What's your view?

The Moral Dimension?

I don't know. I have seen moves overseas, with massive layoffs and plant closures, done to maximize profits. And I have seen it done as a survival strategy, as in Bossidy's story about a move to China. What I have never encountered, aside from the one guy I spoke of earlier, was someone who *enjoyed* the process of lowering costs of doing business with layoffs, closings, and business moves overseas. "Chainsaw Al" Dunlap, of Sunbeam, reputedly did. I read a lot of his book *(Tough Business)* years ago and have to concede the truth of his urging business leaders to grasp reality and do what has to be done.

I especially liked his disgust with the use of the word *stakeholders* as a trendy substitute for what used to be called *shareowners* in annual reports and other communications. If the employees and surrounding communities don't care enough about a publicly traded business to invest in and support it, they deserve to be off the radar screen. The near-total devotional focus needs to be on those who have bought the stock, in whatever quantities.

But sneering at the pain of those who have been downsized in the interests of greater profits, or even survival of the enterprise, is something I couldn't do, perhaps because I am morally superior— or maybe just soft.

Welch never displayed remorse for doing what needed to be done with plant closings and overseas transfers of work. But he constantly hectored his managers with the need to face reality and be courageous enough to both do the unpleasantness and give those who were displaced "soft landings": "Be generous. We've got the money."

GE was known as "Generous Electric" for years before Welch arrived, and then again when the stock took flight.

Don't Get Me Wrong: Reality Sucks

Reality often *does* suck. It involves human misery, the abandonment of quality standards in the interests of costs and pricing, traumatic amputations of businesses that may have ancient roots and venerable lineages in the company, and the loss of personal friendships and loyalties.

Welch was trying to dump appliances in the 1990s but couldn't get a decent price. Koreans are notoriously tough bargainers.

Immelt would love to get rid of appliances as well, but instead he's spending a billion dollars to modernize the division, something he has said he hates to do. But reality dictates that the alternative is to lose big in the marketplace to international players and then be forced into a fire sale down the road.

Bossidy told me that, when writing their book *Confronting Reality*, he and Charan heard advice from several people that their chapter on reality might be better and more mellifluously named "Embracing Reality" than "Confronting" it. But that would be misleading, and they chose against it. Reality is often an ugly, wart-covered, pock-marked bum with fetid breath, one that will get your kids beaten up at school and your spouse angrily confronted at book club or soccer practice.

No, reality is often a disagreeable, smelly pig that must be confronted, kissed (gagging allowed), and taken to whatever dance its squeals indicate is appropriate.

You can avoid meeting this pig in several ways, but all of those are injurious to your business or your career.

One, in particular, is ingesting predigested information fed to you by subordinates who do not want to "fart in church" with unpleasant truths or throw open the door and let the sometimes freezing winds of reality blow in.

Most people's proclivity is to say, "Great job, Sue," when some supporting mythology or cheerleading is supplied. The organization wants to support the boss (you) and is not merely being disingenuous by doing so. They wave the little red books in Maoist fashion and filter the data to match the book or "game plan."

The layers of bureaucracy, at whatever level, tend to feed leaders, at whatever level, with information from the same conventional, favorable, or obsolescent view.

Every layer distorts reality, sometimes slightly or sometimes radically. The nuclear power people at GE were predicting reactor orders that ranged from wishful thinking, to Pollyannaish, to delusional, to "Cargo Cult."

Welch and I used to compare management layers to sweaters worn by a leader. The more sweaters he or she wore, the more difficult it was to discern how cold it was outside or how hard, or from which direction, the wind was blowing.

(Welch and I once argued about who had come up with the "sweaters" analogy. It was I, but it is not a productive activity for a speechwriter to argue origination, especially with an "ownership" personality like Welch. So I asserted my claim and then shut up. I should have *just shut up.*)

Not that we are dealing with Shakespeare here. But it makes sense, and it's real and true. Layers are an impediment to effective leadership.

Wishful Thinking

Wishful thinking is another predilection of those in danger of losing it.

The quintessence of this type of *faux* thinking, aside from the GE nuclear reactor sales predictions, were the "Five Year Plans" of the Soviet Economy of the 1950s. *Mad* magazine (a staple of my youth and subsequent intellectual development) used to publish cartoons of Soviet commissars with chests full of "Hero" medals, announcing that the Motherland's sixth five-year plan had achieved a "glorious" 25% of its objectives after only nine years. In celebration, the chairman had announced a new Five Year Plan.

Some of the strategic planning rituals and underlying philosophy so beloved by corporate America are not too distant from the Soviet model, as if reality could be captured between the pages of slick vinyl books. That kept some of them (not all) comfortably distant from reality and feeling fully in control of events.

Fear is yet another suppressor of reality. In companies where leaders punish people whose views are uncongenial, where contrarian views are seen as an evidence of "bad attitude," fear often prevents people from saying "the wrong thing" (even though it may be the right thing, or the true thing) at meetings or even in casual conversations around the building.

You may have seen the *New Yorker* cartoon in which a stern-faced executive is sitting behind a desk with a cringing underling in front. The big shot says, "Now, I want your candid, straightforward, and possibly career-ending opinion on this matter."

At GE, there used to be a table in the cafeteria where seven or eight mid- to fairly senior managers dined on the subsidized fare (which was excellent). They had a rule: no discussions of "company stuff." But they soon got a reputation for being "cynics," questioners and ridiculers of company initiatives and pronouncements.

They were all friends, and I would join them at times at their "Table of Broken Dreams," as they called it. I did this rarely because I had been warned away from dining with them by a senior HR guy or two who described the table as "radioactive." Besides, I liked to read the paper and eat by myself.

Bossidy used to describe people like them as "the whispering cynics around the water cooler."

Welch quickly became aware of the existence of this table. He knew all of them and possibly misunderstood the function of their dining sessions as being a cynical dissection of company programs and policies. Once again, discussions of company programs and policies were not permitted at the table, by mutual agreement.

These men and woman could have been crushed like bugs— and would have been in a company that punished people with "bad attitudes."

But at GE, it was never done.

These people were (and are) highly intelligent and cynical, as most intelligent people are, and Welch knew that. He bridled under what he heard were their cynical appraisals of some company programs and pronouncements. But he valued them as yet another reality check for many of the things he did or was planning.

He would ask me once in a while, "What are those guys at that table—they're your friends, aren't they?—saying about this or that?" Or, "What will their view be when we launch Six Sigma?"

And I would say, "How the hell should I know? I don't eat at that table. But, yes, they are my friends."

Despite the radioactivity of the table (people carrying their lunch trays with Geiger counters clicking gave it a wide berth—I exaggerate, of course), the "whispering cynics" had good careers, were well paid, and were valued by Welch for their cynicism and insights because they were faithful GE people. To be honest, a couple of them probably would have had better careers had they not been seen as contrarians and cynics, but they managed to do well and remained true to themselves.

A potentially doomed leader will block out negative feedback and even actively discourage it. The "emperor with no clothes" is one of the hoariest bromides around but one of the truest.

Leaders need to stay in touch with opinion at all levels of the company or organization. Rule out stupid people—get rid of them, actually—but listen to the whispering cynics and make sure you let them know that you value them as advisors, even if you reject some (or most) of their views.

Emotion Is Taking Me Over, as Samantha Sang

Passion, self-confidence, and even "swaggering" have always been in the toolkit of a leader, at whatever mid- to senior level he or she may dwell. But they must be tempered—and even shut down completely—as circumstances dictate when they conflict with the iron wall of reality and begin to move the organization in unrealistic or surrealistic directions.

Here's a "for instance."

A business and its leader had achieved temporary greatness by continually improving a breakthrough product through intense R&D expense and efforts. The pages of the *Wall Street Journal* were full of those funny drawings of the CEO. The delightful doe eyes of Maria Bartiromo, the business journalist and now the managing editor of *The Wall Street Journal Report* on CNBC, were fixed on his godlike countenance as he modestly laid out his latest growth projection.

Life was good for him, for his company, and for his shareowners.

But as the slave whispers in the conquering hero's ear, "All glory is fleeting."

And Mark Vachon's sobering question was, "Is this *sustainable?*"

One day, along came a substitute for the company's Holy Grail product.

It may not have been quite as good, but it was still good—and much cheaper.

The customers liked it. It met their needs.

Sales started to drop—and then drop dramatically.

Very often, Golden Boy and his organization can't believe that his "baby" and the organizational meal ticket, the results of so much hard work and creativity, have lost its place in the market.

Eventually, when the writing is on the wall and those numbers defy distorting or ignoring, the organization or the board will "get it." The CEO and most or all of his team will then be escorted out the door.

The image of denying reality that stays in my mind comes from a golf trip to Kiowa Island with some GE friends. After playing our round at one of the great courses, we retired to my friend's beautiful home to hoist some beers and watch the closing round of the British Open.

Denial of reality that led to self-destruction struck a young man named Jean Van de Veide on the 18th hole of the final round of the tournament, held in Scotland in 1999. The tournament awarded a prize of more than a million dollars to the winner.

Van de Veide had a commanding lead. To win the whole thing, he needed only to make a double bogey (two strokes over par for the hole), which was really within the grasp of any "hacker." It was all he had to do for an easy win, to walk away with the pile of money and the global recognition that comes with winning a Major tournament in professional golf.

Not to bore the nongolfers in the readership (if there are either any golfers or any readership), but in this situation, you use relatively short, manageable clubs; keep the ball safely in the fairway; and "hole it out" with a par or bogey (or, in this case, a double bogey) to win the tournament.

That's why viewers all over the world and the spectators at the course in Scotland gasped as he stepped to the tee for the final hole with a driver, the longest and most difficult club to hit with certainty.

It was an insane choice, as viewed by the whole golf world, amateurs included. Van de Veide later claimed his "instinct" told him to do it.

His instinct stunk.

He fought reality—and reality won.

He hit the ball way right, far out of the fairway, but had a lucky "lie" (fluffy setup for the ball, with an easily "makeable" shot back to the fairway).

With another short iron to the green and a putt or two till trophy time.

But his war on reality continued.

Disbelief gripped every one of the millions watching this event as he selected a "two iron," a long and very-difficult-to-hit club, from the bag.

The caddie, who was watching his biggest payday in his life fading, should have hit *him* with the two iron.

Instead, Van de Veide wound up and hit the ball off the clubhouse wall and into some treacherous Scottish rough.

Not to worry.

He then took a wedge, which he should have been using most of the way, and whacked the ball out of the rough—and cleanly into a stream!

He then took off his shoes and socks, and began rolling up his pant legs to wade into the stream and apparently try to hit an underwater ball.

From the dazed, deer-in-the-headlights look on his face, some in the crowd feared he might take his pants *off* and go for a truly golden moment in the history of golf.

By this time, his caddie was stumbling around, with his own big check taking flight over the horizon, and looking like an extra from *The Night of the Living Dead*.

To mercifully end this story, which has become the stuff of golf legend, Van de Veide finally reached in the water and got the ball, took a penalty stroke, dropped, and then hit the ball into a sand bunker.

He wound up making seven on the hole, a triple bogey, and then lost in a sudden-death playoff that never should have happened.

The whole world could see the simple *reality* of what had to be done to win in that tournament, but the leader, the pro, refused to do what reality indicated.

Potential world fame turned into ashes and oblivion.

Reality usually can never be defeated.

Just a Little More on Reality

Not to get too personal, but I ran all the GE meetings—the big ones—for 20 years. One of the perks that came with this was a nice suite at the Boca Raton Hotel and Club in Florida. The biggest meeting, for the top 500 of us in the company, was held there.

I was a bachelor then. I had a wet bar set up in the room, dined on abalone and Dungeness crab legs, struck out with most of the bar waitresses, worked like a dog during the day (with Welch bugging me), and partied fairly hearty late into the night.

They were fun times, and I looked forward to them, except for one awful apotheosis: an evening when, after showering, I was drying my thick, curly hair. The bathroom door, with a full-length mirror, was closed behind me, even though there was no one else in the suite.

As I brushed and dried my mane (not really) in the mirror over the sink, I caught a glimpse in the reflected mirror in the door behind me of a *bald spot* on the back of my head.

It couldn't be!

I think I would have preferred to spot melanoma on my forehead. Genetics had predicted this. But I was only 37 or so and could not accept this. I blanked it out; it was just the way my hair was parted, or some nonsense.

Then I went for a haircut, or "styling," a couple days later at the hotel. I complimented the barber on a good job and gave him a big GE tip. He said, "Yes sir. We got you all covered up on top. Looks good."

"Covered up? What the hell are you talking about?" (Not said aloud.)

But I knew.

As Bossidy and Charan put it in a chapter title, "Reality Bites."

Much later, as a newlywed, I was told by my wife, "Get rid of the comb-over. It looks stupid."

At first I resisted, but I relented when I saw the reality in her view.

The barber said, "Are you sure you want to do this? If I cut this off, I can't put it back."

Do it. Cut off the comb-over. Move to China. Close that product line. Quit that job that you know, in your heart, has no future.

Welch had a comb-over for 20 years or so. When he finally got rid of it, he was officially bald. When I commented about it, he said it was his new "Integrity Cut."

And he was right.

I didn't like it, because I frame people I care for and don't like changes to the portraits within. But I got used to it.

Denial of reality is a non–morally culpable but deadly dangerous violation of what should be your personal standards.

We come back, once again, to Jim McNerney's (of Boeing) view that you must surround yourself with smart people.

And listen to them.

The best advice on the subject of reality came from Laertes' father in *Hamlet:* "To thine own self be true." You know when you are bullshitting yourself—and often when others are bullshitting you.

This advice is repeated in a story shared by Bill Woodburn, a senior executive at GE for years and now the founder of a huge private equity group. Woodburn told me how Welch and several other senior GE people listened to a presentation from a bunch of investment bankers who were pitching a mega-deal that amounted to a hostile takeover (something GE never liked) of a financial services business.

Welch stopped the presentation, laughing, but the message was not laughable.

"Stop the bullshit. I'm 65 years old, and I've seen everything. I've had bullshit coming at me for years, and I know it when I see it coming my way. This is bullshit. Stop it."

Woodburn told me, "The air changed in the room."

The bullshit stopped.

Develop that bullshit detector, whether it's picking up stuff coming from superiors, subordinates, or yourself.

8

Changing Yourself

Changing Your Model

"Reality" may—or should, on occasion—goad you into changing a business model.

Consider the example of Billy Beane, general manager of the Oakland A's, who faced reality in the 1980s. He could not compete with the spending of teams like the Yankees and Red Sox, which were able to field a mega-million-dollar Moose because of the size of their urban and TV markets.

Rather than face a future as an also-ran, Beane sucked up some reality and decided to take a different route. He examined the conventional wisdom that defined which characteristics make a baseball player desirable to a team. His reality-based view was that "getting on base" is the critical component of scoring runs (we're into rocket science here).

His new model did *not* include hiring a quartet of "Mighty Caseys" and a bunch of low-priced bums.

As I understand it, this new business model told Beane that he needed to hire a lot of skillful batters who could take a pitcher deep into late pitch counts, draw walks, make contact, get cheap hits—basically, run up the pitch count and wear the pitcher down.

Using this consciously developed and enforced model, he assembled a team of affordable players and compiled one of the winningest records in baseball.

In 2002, they ranked 12th in payroll and *1st* in the number of games won. The book by Michael Lewis, and now the movie of the same name, *Moneyball,* is based on what they did.

Choose Your Battles

Don't join a bad industry—unless they guarantee you an obscene amount of compensation. Then start looking while still doing the best job you can. You have signed on to the *Titanic* and need to be wearing a life vest and talking with your new best friends, the headhunters.

In their book *Confronting Reality,* Bossidy and Charan pose some specific questions. The first is asking whether you are signing up for what they call "a structurally defective industry" that cannot sustain the cost of capital. Steer clear of these, like Captain Hazelwood's reef, because there is no future in them for you. The party is gonna come to an end no matter how good you are.

Bossidy lists these industries as "reefs": airlines, steel, most automobile manufacturing, rubber, and commodity chemicals. I would add publishing, newspapers, network television, and (for the moment) commercial real estate. (*Note:* If you have a son or daughter with a law degree or MBA, counsel them away from dinosaur industries.)

Larry finished the speech he and I did for his book tour with this advice, which is simple and not at all sophisticated: "Look the realities of your business, or foundation, or whatever, squarely in the eye—be they exciting, or promising, or just plain ugly. Ask yourself the right questions about your situation, your financial goals, your competition, and your direction."

9

Communicate

Talk Less and Listen More

Fifteen or so years ago, my wife and I attended a fete for Jack Welch (for CEO of the Year) at the Hotel Pierre in Manhattan. Ronald Reagan, then just out of office, was the guest speaker. About 150 people were there for dinner and the speech. Reagan filled the room with an aura of "I'm really happy to be talking to you, and I want to do well giving this speech." This wasn't just another $100,000 "show up, throw up" that we'd all witnessed. He did not *want* to get off the podium. He wanted to keep talking to us—to me! "Just let me tell you one more story! Gorbachev told me, on the last day of the Summit...."

Reagan left the podium and walked by our table. My wife claimed I almost tackled him. "We named our daughter after you! We spell it differently—R-e-g-a-n—not quite like yours."

"Really? Thanks," he answered. "Your way is the right way to spell it. My name is a Germanic corruption of the Irish Regan." People were tugging at his sleeve, but this two-term President of the United States only wanted to talk to us. I felt like it was for several minutes; my wife says much less. But I will never forget it, and neither will she.

Have you ever "pitched" someone and seen the glazed-over, dead shark eyes of someone who doesn't care for what you have to say, thinks you're an unimportant fool, has an impending tee time, and isn't listening to a word you're saying? Would you grunt up the hill and charge that machine gun nest for someone like that?

That doesn't mean you should sit down and listen endlessly to blabber from fools.

In a small meeting, perhaps one-on-one or with a couple other people, Welch would hang on your every word. Sometimes I perceived it as a prosecutorial opportunity, with his eyes narrowed as a mongoose follows the movement and vibes of a cobra.

But Welch wasn't bored. And he *was* listening. If you were any good, regardless of your rank, he would hear something that he either liked or hated and would run around the room with it at high decibel. He'd turn the whole presentation into a food fight that would leave you elated when you left. Whether he liked your idea or not, you had challenged him with an idea worthy of his steel. You had distinguished yourself from the throng of nervous, jargon-spewing reciters of "reports," and you had delivered to him a gift—a well-thought-out, passionately articulated case for change of some kind—a warning, a glimpse of an opportunity, a different way of looking at something.

Once you have articulated yourself in this way, whether you're an intern or a vice president, the reaction you provoke will ensure that you will never again relapse into corporate, military, political, legal *droning*. Learning one or two basic and simple tenets of successful communications will, virtually instantly, enable you to distinguish yourself from the pack of smart and hungry people who just do not understand how important this is.

Total Skin, Total Communications

To restate, my nonhumble view is that the ability to interact and communicate effectively is key in *any* profession, line of work, or leadership role. It is critical in just about anything that requires a brain and the ability to lead.

Dr. David Leffell agrees.

Dr. Leffell is quite probably the premier dermatologist in the world (no exaggeration). He practices out of Yale, is heavily published, and is a guest on the big network morning shows. He wrote a book called *Total Skin* that is actually understandable, conversational, and excellent.

He's been carving up my face and body for 20 years. He's also dermatologist to Welch, who left his previous dermatologist because of his lack of communications skills, not because of any defects in his method of practicing medicine.

Dr. Leffell's primary criterion for the aspiring dermatologists he trains at Yale? "First thing is patient interaction. I can teach a monkey to sew."

How does he communicate complex and frightening information to regular, scared people? He tries to understand where the patient is coming from. "You are not adding anything by saying, 'By the way, Mrs. Jones, this might be a melanoma," he says.

Mrs. Jones would just glaze over and panic.

Think of everything said here as applicable to every conversation one has in business—or even in life. That may sound pretentious, but it's true.

The moment you lapse into self-absorption and start disrespecting the poor guy sitting at the table before you, you lose. Your medical business may succeed, but you're no longer succeeding in your profession.

Dr. Leffell told me, "People color everything they hear with their own experience. A patient with basal cell carcinoma so minor she can't remember where it was is different from one whose mother had a basal cell as well and lost her nose."

Dr. Leffell teaches his interns and acolytes to look people in the eyes, shake hands, and speak clear sentences devoid of jargon and lingo. And the moment a patient starts getting "that glazed look," they need to pull back and ask, "Am I not being clear?"

Patients (like business presentees) tend to shut down, according to Dr. Leffell. He gently advises patients dealing with some serious stuff to bring someone else with them. Spouses are okay, but anyone with a brain is fine as well. Women tend to understand medical talk, "wound care," and similar topics better than men, he says.

The main question most people have is, "Doc, am I gonna live?"

But be careful. Saying, "Bring your wife (or husband) along when we talk about this tomorrow" makes people's faces go cold because they suddenly understand the importance of this. That's okay. Sugarcoating isn't advisable—or even ethical.

My late roofing contractor, diagnosed with pancreatic cancer, broke my heart as he staggered around on my roof, weak from chemo. He told me he knew he was "in deep shit" when the doctor told him to bring his wife with him the next day. What kind of man knows he's dying and wants to make sure a virtual stranger's roof is fixed before he becomes too weak?

"Bring your spouse" is a scary signal—but it's unavoidable and must be done with gentleness and hope if there is any chance of being cured.

Two of my dear friends were told to report to the doctor when the wife was diagnosed with particularly invasive breast cancer. The doctor, a woman, led off the cheery conversation with this statement: "I would not go out and plan a funeral at this point, but this is very, very serious."

My friends recalled later that they asked themselves, "Did I just hear what I thought I heard?"

The rest of the conversation was a blur for them.

Jargon and thoughtless communication ruin much of the effectiveness of doctors. It can destroy businessmen and -women. As Bob Galvin says, "De-jargonize your communications."

De-jargonize your life.

My wife and I volunteer at a soup kitchen in Bridgeport, Connecticut, every week. We do stuff like serve salads, dole out soup, and (my particular strong point and function) clean out the 40-gallon stainless-steel soup pot, which the cook fills with whatever is available and produces something that is quite good usually every time. (Quote from one of the guests: "Are we having soup again? Just because this is a 'soup kitchen' shouldn't mean we have to eat this shit every day.")

A lot of eclectic stuff gets thrown into the soup pot. One of the other volunteers emerged from the pantry a year or so ago with a dead mouse that he had trapped a night or two before. The cook, a lovely Jamaican woman, fixed an interested gaze on the late mouse as I was running around the kitchen with mock alarm, shouting, "Stop her! That thing's going in the soup!"

We are volunteers and "nonprofessionals," in this context. A staff of paid "case workers" deals with our "guests," many of whom are substance abusers and are impoverished or homeless. And some of them are among the nicest people I have ever met.

A few of them have a positive attitude toward life that I would kill to own.

I asked the director of the kitchen (and its associated services) a couple years ago for her thoughts on communicating effectively, for another book I was writing.

Her view was that, when you finish the rehearsal of any of your important communications, you *must* ask the people who listened to you, "What did you hear me say?" Their answer will be something that *is totally opposite* of what you wanted to convey. You *must* correct this.

Toxic Jargon

Doctors don't dissemble with each other, except maybe, in business matters. For medical matters, they speak in code (argot)—but it is *understood code*. Shorthand.

And that's okay. It saves time.

Jargon does *not* save time in other professions or across functions. It bores, annoys, and wastes the time of people who have better, more productive things to do. It makes them hate you—and the jargon and buzzwords—even if they themselves use them.

Jargon is infectious and inflammatory, and it's corrosive to your communications ability and the way your peers view you.

Lightweights think jargon makes them sound sophisticated and businesslike. Real leaders, including CEOs, restrain themselves from using jargon and buzzwords. These words have *phony* and *poseur* written all over them.

Most buzzwords began as insightful, even lyrical descriptions of human and business behavior. But then they get degraded, prostituted, ridiculed because of overuse. The fact is, people realize the one who's using them is unable to formulate a coherent thought without a lot of rhetorical props stolen from the guy who originated them years ago.

Who invented the phrase "at the end of the day"? Way back when, it was an original and evocative phrase. But it has been so degraded from overuse that its endless repetition, often nonsensically out of context, marks the speaker as a kind of pompous empty suit who's incapable of expressing himself in his own words.

Political talk shows feature cretins repeating it endlessly. I have to leave the room—or be asked to leave it by my long-suffering wife.

In *Jacked Up*, I detail something called Bullshit Bingo. It reportedly originated at Oxford or some other university in England, a country that values its language and laughs at its degradation more than most. That game of Bullshit Bingo emigrated to Harvard's business school. To play, scores of students were given bingo-style matrixes with business clichés arranged in the various boxes (as numbers, I guess, are arranged in bingo games).

I don't play bingo and hope not to for a few years—hopefully, not until death approaches.

At Harvard, when a notoriously, boring speaker (some CEO or a business academic) stepped up to the lectern to expel an ill-prepared, rambling, self-serving homily, the matrixes were stealthily distributed and the fun began.

Parents were paying $75,000 or more a year for this playtime. But it wasn't the kids' fault. In fact, they were actually learning as they played it.

When I wrote about it last time, the bromides on the Bullshit (or Buzzword) Bingo board included *proactive, bandwidth, pushback, drill down, no-brainer,* and *24/7.* Many of them have held up.

If you use these jargon words and phrases as "Hamburger Helper"—that is, filler or repetitive transitions in your addresses to people—either orally or in writing, the antennae on the smarter people among your listeners will start twitching, whether they're employees, customers, or constituents. We call people who use these phrases with regularity "Jargon Monkeys." We look down on them and demean them because they seem to be betraying a lack of original thought. That is, in fact, what the Oxford pioneers of this learning game thought repetitive jargon mongering to be.

In my experience, reciting buzzwords and clichés is a "tag" for lower intelligence. It is not a tag for *low* intelligence—just the lower intelligence that does not typically produce six- to seven-figure incomes—at least, not for long. Jargon words and phrases are career-retarders, if not destroyers. Welch used to rail about what he called "busineese" and "terms," and he'd sneer at the people who used them with regularity.

An Unarguably Provocative Presentation

Massachusetts Sen. Charles Sumner made an effective presentation on the floor (literally, when it was over) to the United States Senate in May 1856. In my pathetic and ultimately failed postulations as a PhD candidate in American History in 1979, my view was that his speech, and the reaction to it, represented the point of no return in the American rush to the greatest bloodbath in our history.

In his "Crime Against Kansas" pitch, Sumner ridiculed the "aristocracy" of the South and mocked what he viewed (accurately) as the two chief defenders of the migration of that "peculiar institution" to Kansas (also known as "bleeding Kansas" because of the visceral and understandable violence over the slavery issue). One of the senators Sumner mocked was Stephen Douglas of Illinois, who was quite famous at the time; the other was Sen. Andrew Butler of South Carolina.

Butler, who had some kind of neurological disorder (possibly a stroke) was ridiculed in the speech for his "slurring utterances." Sumner trashed the whole of South Carolina and the South itself for its "aristocratic" pretensions.

This guy was cruising for a beat-down.

Butler wasn't present at the time of Sumner's "presentation." But Douglas was, and he whispered to a colleague during it, "This damn fool is going to get himself shot by some other damn fool."

Fairly prophetic, if imprecise, in choice of weaponry.

The speech was hugely reviewed.

But the reviews were mixed, depending on where you lived.

One of the most graphic and dramatic "reviews" was provided by Congressman Preston Brooks of South Carolina. Brooks walked with a "gutta-percha" (a preplastic, natural, inelastic tree product) cane with a gold head, which he wielded because of a gunshot wound to the hip he had suffered in a duel a few years earlier.

These were some serious dudes.

In any case, on May 22, 1856, three days after the senator's historic speech, Congressman Brooks strolled into the chamber of the United States Senate, accompanied by another congressman, Laurence Keitt.

The chamber was nearly empty.

Senator Sumner was writing quietly at his desk, perhaps crafting a new speech, when Congressman Brooks approached him. He said, "Mr. Sumner, I have read your speech twice over carefully. It is a libel on South Carolina and Mr. Butler, who is a relative of mine."

Brooks was a picture of barely controlled fury, which Sumner apparently sensed. He began to stand up from his desk, which had only one open side and was bolted to the floor.

Brooks apparently felt that Sumner's speech had demonstrated that he was full of shit. He proceeded to beat it out of him, raining blows from the cane on the man, mostly on his head. The beating was so severe that Sumner apparently sensed that death was at hand if he didn't do something. With the strength born of desperation, he ripped the desk out of its floor bolts and tried to flee, blinded by his blood. Brooks followed him with a hail of blows, beating him into unconsciousness; he continued beating him until his cane disintegrated into splinters.

Brooks then sauntered defiantly out of the Senate chamber, accompanied by Congressman Keitt, who had waved a pistol at those who seemed ready to stop this attack, and shouted, "Let them be!" (as if Sumner was a willing participant in this combat).

Sumner became an invalid because of the beating and remained out of the Senate for three years. He returned, after Brooks had died "of croup," to become an even more bloodthirsty warmonger and hater of the South.

Brooks survived an expulsion vote in the House and was deluged with dozens of canes sent from Southerners by mail, to replace his splintered one. One had the inscription "Good Job."

Towns and counties in the South were named after him. The *Richmond Enquirer* felt that the attack was an act "good in conception, better in execution, and best of all in consequences."

Nice.

Sumner was revered as a hero and near-martyr among abolitionists across the North.

In my view—and one that coincides with the view of most historians—civil war was nearly inevitable at this point, almost five years before Ft. Sumter.

The momentum toward war was not impeded by the dithering of a very distant relative of mine, James Buchanan (whose "First Lady" was his niece, Harriet *Lane*).

Weird.

Sumner's presentation was arguably successful and certainly provocative. In thinking it over as the bones in his head kneaded, though, Sumner may have wished he'd used some different phrasing in some passages.

He had used no cliché: It was a great and forceful presentation of views, no one had been bored by it, and no one had failed to get the point. My first boss at GE, a great man and a talented communicator who headed the speechwriters shop, told us repeatedly, "Never attack the audience." I think I agreed with him then. I don't now, and since he's no longer around, he won't contest my view.

If the "audience" *deserves* to be attacked or upbraided do it. Any Army or Marine drill instructor will tell you that.

My view is that the maxim should be, "Never bore the audience." Don't hose them down with borrowed, shopworn, business clichés. As I've said, Welch used to gag at them. And I, in the back of the room at the meetings I ran for him, used to cringe when I heard them.

But back to my off-point [cliché] message: Charles Sumner may have precipitated the Civil War with his attack on South Carolina and the South itself. The war may have been inevitable anyway, but the speech crystallized a thought and provoked a reaction.

How many business or other institutional presentations you've heard provoke *anything* other than Blackberry usage, snoring, and bathroom trips? Bullshit artists—or "feather merchants," as we used to call them at the Pentagon—never hit the higher rungs and are often relegated to the lesser circles of the bureaucracy. Once again, if you make incredible amounts of money for your company or have led your organization to striking success, you can stand up and babble and ramble without getting tossed.

You will get paid well, but you will seldom ascend to the top rung.

Losing It in One Easy Presentation

It *can* happen—less so at the very senior levels, more so at the midsenior levels, and very much so at the lower management

levels. I have seen only a few careers destroyed at senior management levels by awful presentation skills. I have seen more destroyed
or set back by one, poorly prepared, rambling, artless, and useless
presentation.

Here's how to do it, how to lose it in one effortless business
presentation.

Don't Prepare

I have credibility here. Years ago, I pursued a PhD degree at
American University in Washington, D.C., while working at the
Pentagon. I put in almost four intense years of study of the pre–
Civil War era, and the presidency of James K. Polk. I completed
my course work with distinction and began to study for the written
comprehensive examinations that followed. I curtailed my social
life dramatically. I spent nights and weekends at the Library of
Congress and was known by name to the staff. I wrote the series
of three or four of the five-hour exams and passed them all, one
or two with "distinction." The remaining hurdle, before I was permitted to begin my doctoral dissertation, was an oral introduction
and questioning by the senior history faculty. My advisor, a friend,
assured me that this would be no big deal after my superior performance on the "writtens." He told me not to worry about it: "You'll
do fine." With that advice (the worst I have ever been given), I
began another two months of preparation, but this time without
nearly the effort and intensity that had characterized my previous
work.

I stood in front of the panel of examiners on the appointed
afternoon and began to answer their questions. I began to experience the terrifying despair that came as I flubbed the first few. The
air in the room began to change, and the interaction went from
friendly and collegial to worried and grim. Hardly anyone ever
failed the predissertation oral, but I could feel in my cold face that

I was working on it. They gave me every opportunity to redeem myself, but I was simply not prepared. After about 45 minutes, I was asked to excuse myself from the room so they could deliberate, which they did briefly. Then they called me back to deliver the verdict as gently as they could: I "did not pass," had shown a "lack of preparation for the examination," and "should take another few months of study before appearing before them again."

I nodded, thanked them quietly, and walked in a trance down the hall of the history building, noticing that the office doors that had lined the hall were closing before me as I walked toward the exit. Word had apparently spread, that I had botched the exam, and no one in the offices wanted to make eye contact in my progress toward the Exit sign.

I never went back. All those years of work wasted, and I had nothing to show for them except an iron resolve to *never, ever be unprepared for any presentation or session important to me, as long as I lived.* Please learn from my humiliation and failure, never allow it to happen in your professional life.

That describes what will happen and how it will feel in a typical business presentation setting if you needlessly fail and lose it.

Again, Don't Prepare

You've been told you have to do a pitch at an analyst meeting, or a company meeting, or the morning meeting, in front of your boss and colleagues. Don't think about what your colleagues or boss might need to know—stuff that could help them. Just hit the PowerPoint or dredge up some old filler from some file and crank out a bunch of self-serving word charts on everything you know. Twenty or 30 of those, and you're loaded for bear! (Or *bare*, actually, since you will be displaying your bare and uninteresting ass for all to see, and laugh at, later.)

Don't Rehearse

Are you kidding me? It's boring. Make a guess at how long the pitch will take when you actually stand up and hear yourself do it.

Don't Take It Seriously

Start by saying whatever comes into your head as the AV guy is trying to figure out why the show won't run off your laptop. (You would have had to miss either cocktail hour last night or breakfast, this morning to do a test run.) You're kind of hung over, so you laugh a lot as all this is going on and say some "funny" things to your audience.

Act as if this is no big deal. They'll be honored, especially the people in the crowd who are compiling mental and written notes on you—which have *already* been filed under "Lightweight."

Take a Big Dump

Deliver a lot of boring background and analysis intended to show how smart you are and how much work you've done on whatever it is you do rather than telling them *right away* why what you are about to tell them might be useful and important to them, not to you.

Telegraph: Boring. Boring. Aooga! Aooga! Dive, Dive for the Blackberries and iPhones!

Say stuff like, "Later on in my presentation, I'll get into much more detail on the 15 factors we analyzed as part of Project X, but first let me give you an overview and some detailed background on how my team approached this project when we began less than two years ago." To the AV guy: "Can you help me again with this thing?

I can't get off this title screen. God, I hope I do better with this spacebar than I did with my golf game yesterday afternoon. Okay, I think I've got it now. Is that it? Are you sure? Okay, here we go...." (*Telegraphed message:* Do not drive or operate heavy machinery while listening to the following presentation.)

Throw Up a Bunch of "Eye Charts"

Suspect that your busy PowerPoint word charts may be unreadable to at least some (likely most) of the people in the room, but wisely conclude that no one will bother reading them anyway. No need to clean them up. You can always say, "I know this is a little bit of an eye chart...heh, heh." They will understand. This is the way lightweight losers and journeyperson PowerPoint junkies speak to each other.

"Visualize" Everything

Make sure there's a chart on the screen for every single moment of the pitch, whether one is necessary or not. Don't dare to simply look people in the eyes and passionately tell them something that you believe is important to know, with a blank screen behind you. How weird would that be?

Show 'Em Your Ass

Plant your backside in the audience's face, look intently at the screen, and read whole "bullets" while embellishing them with spontaneous projectile-vomiting of data that no one cares about and will never remember. They will probably try intently to *not* remember it, if that doesn't get in the way of their increasing resolve to hate you.

Lull the Cobras to Sleep

If you, by chance, happen to glance at the audience, note the vacant eyes, yawns, and increasingly obvious PDA use. Understand, as your presentation slogs toward the midpoint, that they have already finished their routine email and are now sending messages back and forth across the room to each other, confessing suicidal and homicidal thoughts. You will be able to note them smirking and smiling ruefully at each other across the room. But screw them. Push on anyway and continue to drive these poor bastards through data that is of no use to them. After all, you spent a lot of your time on this (on the data, not the presentation). Notice your boss, fixing a gaze of intense boredom, exasperation, and contempt upon you.

Become Comically Panicky

Your lack of preparation and self-absorbed rambling have left you 20 minutes over your time limit, and you have 11 more charts to cover before you get to your closing rehash. Shift into warp-speed reading of your unreadable word charts. Ignore the laughter and groans from the victims who are being PowerPoint-boarded and would prefer to be in Gitmo.

Pepper Your Presentation with the Latest Jargon and Business Buzzwords

Say things like "It's a no-brainer" and the Gregorian chant "at the end of the day" at least once a minute, even though the people who can influence your career and are suffering through this corporate horseshit think that *you* are a no-brainer and plainly wish that "the end of the day" (or the end of their lives, or yours) had already occurred.

Understand and Accept

You didn't really prepare your presentation—you threw together 35 charts as crib sheets and got up and bullshitted from them. It's not a prepared, polished, pointed piece of work. It's lazy oral dysentery, and everyone knows it. They will leave the room with a little piece of their lives wasted by you, empty-handed, intensely bored, and resentful. And if they ever get a chance to influence anything that influences *your* career, they will remember that you contributed nothing to furthering their own.

Wonder Why

As you careen to a useless, muddy, rambling rehash of a conclusion, and the crowd runs out of the place like it was on fire, wonder why your career isn't progressing as rapidly as you once thought it might. And wonder why you are *losing it*.

I've watched this for more than 30 years, and I swear that making a business presentation is an easily acquired skill that you neglect at the risk of career retardation or even career death.

10

The Final Word

Let me partly shut up and let John Samuels, one of the smartest and most accomplished of the GE senior team (and that's saying something, like one of the better hitters on the New York Yankees) relay from his yellow pad in his office some of the things I asked him to ponder before we met for this book.

On Accountability

"If you are running a large public company, your board of directors, which is supposed to be overlooking you, is seldom 'hands-on.' You could miss some numbers, lose share, lose competitiveness and continue to ride around in your jet, go to charity events, and you were fine. You had to practically run the company 'into a ditch' to get canned. If you run a business at GE and you 'miss,' you have a swarm of big staff people all over you, asking questions, giving 'suggestions'—and possibly suggestions that you clear out your desk, if you do not implement them." The individual businesses at GE have, in essence, two boards of directors: the one with its pictures in the annual report, and the gimlet-eyed and talented corporate staff.

Beware of Loyalty

What do you think is the number-one quality that most leaders want in the top leaders that work for them? Some say intelligence, integrity, expertise, diligence, and so on. I think the most common view is that *loyalty* trumps all. It's a human desire. But people don't like to get bad news, so "loyal" lieutenants may "spin" it: They put lipstick or rouge on something putrid. They aren't quite the yes-men (or women), but their "loyalty" isn't helping you.

"The people you want around you," says Samuels, "are people who don't need the job—people who have self-confidence." I would add, at the senior levels, that you want people who have "screw-you money," who love what they are doing, and who love you, in a way.

"You want men and women at the senior levels who would run up the hill for you and take the bullets for you, and you only get them if they know that you really care about them, and their careers, and their families. Arrogant and autocratic behavior prevents that belief," Samuels says.

Let me interject here: I've worked with Jack Welch on a number of occasions when one of his top guys or gals has gotten back to him from the hospital or their homes while recovering from prostate, or heart, or breast cancer surgery, or some sad, serious illness of one of their family members. Welch was immensely comforting and always quick with some variation of "What do you need? What can I do? Sloan Kettering? Cleveland Clinic? Just lemme know." He'd then get off the phone, shaken by the troubles, and describe the pain the person was in. He'd shudder a few times, and then we'd get back to work. His people, at every level of the company, including mine and even lower, knew this was not fakery—possibly a bit of Irish sentimentality, but affectionate regard for people whom he *held in regard*.

Samuels says "the number-one quality you should want is *candor.*"

Cultivate it. Welcome the harsh criticism of a direct report, even if it pisses you off so much that you want to rip his or her heart out—even if you are sure the comment is probably worthless. Squash it in a rage, and the tortoise will withdraw the head into the shell. And the "head" is what you are paying for and must cherish and cultivate.

Samuels quotes a Japanese business proverb: "None of us is as smart as all of us.

Warren Buffett's View

Warren Buffet had a novel but instructive view of success and failure at all levels of enterprise: "He didn't measure his managers on straight returns."

Samuels asked him, at a GE meeting (Welch and Buffet were pals and still are), "Wait a minute. How do you decide if they're any good?"

Buffett said, "Every year I ask them the same question: 'Is the moat between you and your competition getting bigger or smaller? If it's widening, you are going to grow share and price. If it is narrowing, you have a problem.'"

Samuels avers that the key, what we want from our managers, is, "We are looking for a long-term, sustainable advantage.

"That's how managers get in trouble: They look for how to make this year's quarter, or 'number.'"

The Passionlessness of the Crust

Now back to me. In my youthful speechwriting days, pre-Welch, I occasionally worked for a reasonably young, handsome, and fairly accomplished senior vice president at a GE location in the South.

Trips down there to work with him on a "talk" afforded me an opportunity to visit my beloved Washington and see a female friend I had been dating when seduced by the siren song of Generous Electric and brought to what I thought of as the boring, frigid wastes of Connecticut.

The man for whom I was writing the speech was very pleasant. He liked me and talked of "fixing me up" with his daughter, whom I never met.

But on one occasion I will never forget, he reviewed a speech I did for him in the presence of his "communications guy," a wonderful young man and a former great baseball player who was in the final throes of multiple sclerosis. The man had trouble speaking and fell down repeatedly while walking. His shoes were a scuffed disaster.

In any case, the vice president was good to him and kept him on (in a fairly senior job) out of basic, benevolent, human instincts and a respect for his ardor for doing a good job and for his high intelligence.

That day, he and I sat down with the vice president, who had read the speech I had prepared and liked it, but he felt it was not "businesslike" enough. "Why don't we take it in a little bit different direction?" In other words, we could include some odious stuff from an industry report that made me want to jump out the window. My poor friend (now long dead) agreed that it was a ruinous assault on a good talk, with a point. But he didn't do it as vociferously as I wound up doing.

Then the boss said, "And I think we need some slides. Remember [directed at his communicator] that one with the graph and the bullets on the [disguised] industry?"

I went nuts—or as nuts as a 35-year-old speechwriter can go with a senior vice president at GE.

"This is boring. And they will *think* it's boring. Why do you want to make it boring?"

The boss shut me down gently. "Bill, I know it will be boring. But that's what this group expects, so I'll get up and bore them."

This guy's people, and the people across GE, had been wearing T-shirts with a slogan I'd come up with that essentially turned out to be hyperbolic nonsense. The business underperformed, and the boss was removed.

Not my fault. Or maybe partly my fault for overselling something (factory automation) in which I believed, perhaps naively, but totally and passionately.

At this point in my career, I wasn't even thinking of hitching a wagon to a star. I was already Welch's semiofficial speechwriter, so when Welch interrupted a conversation with me to take a call from a vice chairman and returned to the subject of this business by saying, "This guy is going to be out of this job in a few months," I felt bad because I liked him.

But I understood.

The passion has to be there! "I'll get up and bore them," you say? And work with that view, for a guy named Welch?

Goodbye.

Welch never lost the fire, the passion. I see him on TV now, and he still has it. In fact, he has begun to stutter just a bit, as he used to do in what Dennis Dammerman, his CFO, has called his "violent period," a phrase that never ceases to make me laugh. When the stuttering and stammering began in a one-on-one conversation or at a small conference-table meeting, the alarm bells would go off. You knew the shit was about to hit the fan—or you.

The intensity, the passion would escalate to a boil, seldom directly abusive to an individual. It was often wildly positive and full of promise, and something that I call *amor fou* (stealing from the French phrase that Tony's shrink uses in *The Sopranos*).

Crazy love.

Listen to some of the language, most of it from his CEO annual report letters, which, in other companies, are usually sedative devices for insomniacs:

"Bureaucracy is the Dracula of institutional behavior, and will rise again and again, requiring everyone in the organization to reflexively pound stakes through its reappearances." (I wanted the stake to be pounded through its heart, but Jack reigned me in.)

Or:

"We cultivate a hatred of bureaucracy in our Company and never for a minute hesitate to use that awful word 'hate.' Bureaucrats must be ridiculed and removed."

Or:

"The top 20% and middle 70% (of managers, or perhaps employees in general) are not permanent labels. However, the bottom 10%, in our experience, tend to remain there. A company that bets its future on its people must remove that lower 10% and keep removing it every year—always raising the bar of performance and increasing the quality of its leadership."

Not enough. Sports teams do better than that. And we never really removed 10%, but the overstatement, and the passion that drove it, got the point across that nonperformers could no longer be tolerated anywhere in the company.

Or:

"There are undoubtedly a few 'type IV's (successful, but nasty, oppressive, and tyrannical managers) remaining, and they must be found." (Scary, but documented in the case of some successful senior managers who did not share or implement the values of the company, values at which we had arrived after serious month's-long debate and deliberation.)

These values were not from some hyperbolic mission statement concocted by a PR firm. I've been out of the company for nine years and still carry my values card in my ratty old wallet.

Attack Good News: Do Not Tolerate It Without Explanation!

Lloyd Trotter recounted for me, with amusement in his voice, "You must question the good news." He spoke of taking over a fairly sizable GE business after its previous captain walked the plank.

At an early meeting in his new job, he "went around the room" with the senior people in the components of his new business.

"So let me know about how things are going and our prospects."

Nirvana!

"Great. Things are going well. Big plans. Terrific."

Unanimous!

This sounded fishy to Trotter, and he went around the room again after this preface: "Look, the guy I am replacing just got *fired* because of bad results. And now you all tell me that everything is great and getting better. What's changed? I need to know *because I don't want to get fired.*"

They opened up, describing their segments, warts and all, and left out the rouge and powder during future briefings.

"Pick apart 'success stories'—and *projected* success stories," says Trotter. (And there are a lot of the latter out there.)

Trotter told me of some effusive calls that came into his business from a big customer about a GE individual's performance in keeping him out of trouble and satisfying him. Business leaders love that kind of stuff and think warmly of the individual being feted. After a couple such messages, however, Trotter was overcome with curiosity and called the big customer himself. He asked, "Should I be happy about this?" Turns out that the customer was just nervously joyous that the GE guy had rectified a "mess that should not have been made in the first place."

Says Trotter, "When an individual or unit is succeeding wildly, you must ask, 'How, *specifically*, was this done?'"

Bill Woodburn says, "When things go well, we tend to look away and enjoy it. We go into our 'end-zone dance' and celebrate."

You must continue to "drill down," as the annoying and overused cliché goes, until you are satisfied that you understand exactly how these miracles were performed.

Boring but Pertinent Sports Stories and Analogies

I began this mini-tome with an inspiring (to me) story about how Tom Coughlin dragged himself and his New York Giants back from oblivion and, in 2008, beat the undefeated New England Patriots in the Super Bowl. It was possibly the greatest Super Bowl game in history (depending on from where you're from).

It inspired me because it seemed to prove that someone on the verge of losing changed himself; he saved himself by removing from himself the *arrogance* that Jim McNerney says is at the root of all "flame-outs."

I'm glad I didn't write the book more quickly, because Coach Coughlin fell off the arrogance wagon in the 2010 season and missed the all-important playoffs with two horrible losses toward the end of the season. In one loss to the Philadelphia Eagles, the Giants were up by 21 points, with eight minutes to go.

Giants fans were smugly high-fiving each other and heading for the exits, hoping to cut the three-hour-average nightmare on the Jersey Turnpike and, in my case, the Cross Bronx Expressway, "Hutch," and Merritt Parkway, to two hours. I was with my son and was almost getting ready to leave when something bothered me about the way they were playing, despite the lead. So we stuck around to watch the Giants *lose* as a result of poor play and horrible coaching decisions.

We walked and rode the escalator out of the stadium, past Giant fans beating the hell out of overlording Eagle fans. We heard people wailing, sometimes to themselves, "How did this happen? Tell me this didn't just happen!"

It was the worst disaster in Giants' history. I realize this is just a stupid game, but the point is coming.

Another game, another disaster—bear with me. Then the Giants played the Redskins and won. But with some complicated and boring exigencies of other teams having to beat other teams, the Giants were eliminated from the playoffs.

Tempest in a teapot, I know.

But listen to the newly puffed-up and then deflated coach in the locker room after it was plain that the Giants were going home to golf and other stuff instead of continuing to play football and moving toward a Super Bowl.

Coughlin told his players that anyone not impressed with a 10–6 season could "line up and kiss [his] ass." He delivered those remarks in the visitors' locker room at FedEx Field. To be exact, he said, "Hey, from the bottom of my heart, okay? A ten-season win in the NFL today, okay? They can kiss my ass. Okay? They can line up and kiss my ass."[1]

Uh, excuse me, Coach, am *I* supposed to line up to kiss your ass, when I pay $800 a game for my two seats, which I can't even sell for that price on StubHub? Coughlin then said that there were a few more things he wanted to say, except that a "priest is here."

An exorcist would have been appropriate.

This was a major relapse.

My thought at the time was that he should have quit after the Super Bowl win and the Gatorade bath.

And then he blew up all my theorizing by winning another Super Bowl in February 2012, after giving a speech in which he said he loved every man in that locker room. The stake was driven through the old Coughlin arrogance, perhaps never to return.

If we're arrogant, we seldom get the chance to change and redeem ourselves as he did.

The Luck of Some Irish

You could—and should—make the argument that Welch lucked out, inheriting a beautiful, intensely loyal and familial company with a magnificent balance sheet and a tradition of being the West Point of global business talent development.

But he ran it, whipped it, led it, and taught it to become the paradigm of the world's greatest company. At one point, it was the most valuable company in the world (measured by shares outstanding × share price).

I remember one day in the late 1980s when a short article appeared in one of the New York papers bemoaning the troubles of IBM. It included a sentence or two about Welch. I asked him in the hall if he's seen it, and he asked, with classic Irish fatalism, "Is it bad?" I told him (with uncharacteristic and unintentional ass-kissing, I guess) that he should "laminate this article and wear it around his neck, like a badge."

The article had words to the effect, as the last of the maharajas of IBM were fading from the scene, "Here's to Jack Welch, who saved his company."

Welch would dispute that, because old GE was never in "dire straits," but as our sportswriter wrote, he did harness momentum, energetically "goose" it, and stay out of the way of the dynamism of a bunch of young and not-so-young men and women who were encouraged to rage and roar in a bunch of different markets.

The luck of getting to manage through the good old days of the mid-to-late 1980s and 1990s was fun as well, as opposed to slogging through the muck of the last decade.

I'm not sure if "stayed out of its way" and simply "harnessed momentum" is a totally accurate summary of what he did, as illustrated by my previous vignettes of his swimming at all levels of the company and doing what would be described as micromanaging problems at incredibly low levels that caught his attention or ire. Almost inevitably, he did add value.

The problem with being so good and so charismatic in any job at any level, but especially when you're the CEO, is that if you die, leave, or go to the slammer suddenly, the whole edifice can suffer badly because of its identification with you.

So GE was never a "one-man band," and Welch would have hated having it be thought so. No doubt he took intense pride and satisfaction in the team he had assembled over the years (with a few turkeys flapping along temporarily), so he was content and comfortable to bail out at age 65, despite our partly affectionate and partly greedy entreaties that he stick around for, say, three more years or so.

Sticking around even a little too long can turn an icon into a "has been, needs-to-go." As Woody Allen points out, "Eternity is very long—especially toward the end."

There are generally (but not always) limits to the duration of success. Welch got out with perfect timing, and Buffett seems impervious to longevity-related failure.

Jeff Dworken, global CFO of Ernst and Young, told me, "Very few people have a run that is straight up. The shelf life of leaders is not unlimited."

With the luck of the Irish, Welch "got outta Dodge" not ahead of the sheriff, but less than a week in front of the evil acts of 9/11 that hurt GE and most other major companies.

Dworken says, "Even great people sometimes stick around too long, and the tom-toms start to beat. People get tired and people at levels at which you are trying to drive change often begin to resist. And when you start to hear that, it's time for *you* to change."

My obvious observation is that you can never even *appear* to slow up. At the Pentagon, we used to say that no rabbit ever dies a natural death in the wild. They simply get slower and slower until something kills and eats them.

If you begin to slow up in the midst of your professional life and begin to hear those "tom-toms" or pursuing footfalls, your clock is ticking unless you do something. That point could be, arguably, too late.

Luck may be a factor in your career, but *you* are the master or mistress of your destiny.

Any other view, in *my* view, is the view of one who is losing it—or has lost it.

Be true to yourself. Ask yourself *and your colleagues* whether they ever perceive you as *arrogant,* whether they ever see you wandering near the River Styx of *integrity* violation, whether you are a little behind in what's going on, and whether you need to communicate with them and the people who work for you more frequently, more passionately, and with better skills. Ask them whether you are spending too much time on social stuff and on window dressing for your shop rather than knowing intimately how your shop works from the bottom up.

Ask yourself these and the other questions I have tried to share in this book. They represent the best of 30 years of my observations of leadership and, better, the views of some very accomplished individuals who have made it into the stratosphere and are determined to stay there.

And I have told of those who made it—or almost made it—and lost it.

Don't *you* lose it.

Best of luck to you, whether you need it or not!

Endnote

1. Ohm Youngmisuk, "Tom Coughlin Blasts Critics After Win," ESPN, http://sports.espn.go.com/new-york/nfl/news/story?id=5995021.

Index

FT Press
FINANCIAL TIMES

In an increasingly competitive world, it is quality
of thinking that gives an edge—an idea that opens new
doors, a technique that solves a problem, or an insight
that simply helps make sense of it all.

We work with leading authors in the various arenas
of business and finance to bring cutting-edge thinking
and best-learning practices to a global market.

It is our goal to create world-class print publications
and electronic products that give readers
knowledge and understanding that can then be
applied, whether studying or at work.

To find out more about our business
products, you can visit us at www.ftpress.com.